BEAUTY FOR ASHES

BEAUTY FOR ASHES

Learning from Christ How to Endure
Life's Greatest Pains, Sufferings, and Sorrows

SCOTT A. LIVINGSTON

Covenant Communications, Inc.

Cover image: *The Agony in the Garden* (detail), by Frans Schwartz, Courtesy of the Museum of Art, Brigham Young University. Full image depicted above and on back cover. For more information, visit www.moa.byu.edu.

Published by Covenant Communications, Inc.
American Fork, Utah

Printed in the United States of America
First Printing: September 2015

21 20 19 18 17 16 15 10 9 8 7 6 5 4 3 2 1

ISBN-13: 978-1-68047-634-7

DEDICATION

To Ginger: You loved me perfectly and taught me how.

To my parents: Alan, Neda, Ray, and Bonnie. You always believed.

To my children: Isaac & Anna, McKenzie, Caleb. and Elise. Heaven is kind.

To my brothers and sisters: Cory, Kent, Leslie, Michael, Monica, and Jaylyn. I love you.

To all the friends, disciples, leaders, and mentors that have helped along the path. Thank you for stopping so often to wait for me to catch up. I'm still walking . . .

To my Smashing Story friends: Caleb, Steph, Maleah, James, Melissa, Loraine, Janiel, Maegan, and Cally, each gifted and each the giver of so many gifts. Thank you.

And to the Savior, most of all, for giving me *Beauty for Ashes* and for His enabling grace that I might someday, somehow also become a beautiful one.

TABLE OF CONTENTS

INTRODUCTION

"To give unto them beauty for ashes"—*Isaiah 61:3*

SHE WANTED ME, AS HER bishop, to give her permission to divorce her husband. She'd finally had enough of his emotional abuse, his repeated infidelities, and his chronic selfishness. My "approval" was the final requirement she needed before she took the all-but-inevitable step of ending her marriage.

Such a choice certainly seemed justified. She'd been holding on for years. Trying to keep both her testimony and her family intact while watching her spouse blow up his life had taken a tremendous toll on her physically, emotionally, and spiritually. Her eyes were filled with pain and fatigue as she sat in the quiet of my office. "I can't do it anymore, Bishop. I just want to start over. Before it's too late to start over."

I prayed fervently for direction. I'd never counseled someone to get a divorce or even suggested that such a drastic step was the right course of action. But in this instance it seemed only right to do so. I'd counseled with her husband on several occasions. He was always indifferent, and at times even defiant. My warnings to him that his Church membership was in danger if he chose not to repent held no weight. His reply was simply to "go for it."

He'd never really had a testimony anyway, he told me. Not being a member of the Church would be a relief. That way his wife could no longer hold Church membership, the temple, and the priesthood over his head.

As I pled for heavenly direction, a passage of scripture from the Sermon on the Mount came quietly into my mind. It was not at all what I had expected to hear:

> Ye have heard that it hath been said, Thou shalt love thy neighbour, and hate thine enemy.
>
> But I say unto you, Love your enemies, bless them that curse you, do good to them that hate you, and pray for them which despitefully use you, and persecute you. (Matthew 5:43–44)

Surely that wasn't the answer. Such a response couldn't apply in this particular situation, could it? This good, faithful sister had already tried "loving her enemy," hadn't she? She had prayed for him again and again. Prayed and fasted, even. The Lord couldn't be asking her to do more than she'd already done. Clearly she'd given all that she could give in her efforts to "do good" to one who seemed indeed to be "despitefully using" her, and she'd received only hurt and heartache in exchange.

With no other inspiration to offer, I reluctantly opened my scriptures to the verses I'd felt impressed to share. I was sure she would be shocked by my apparent lack of sensitivity for her situation. Hadn't I been listening? Didn't I understand? Again I prayed, this time even more intently—not for just myself but also for her. If this is your answer, Heavenly Father, please help thy daughter know that it is your answer. As we read the words of the Savior together, the Holy Spirit quietly filled the room. This was her answer. This was the way.

I told her that the Lord was giving her permission to quit trying to change her husband. Only the Lord could do that, and then only with her husband's willingness to change. Instead she should focus on trying to become more like the Savior through her daily, personal strivings. The Lord would bless her for it, and would help her to know what else He wanted her to do in relation to her marriage. Divorce was not, at least for now, her answer. She nodded at me through her tears, meekly thanked me, and left my office. My drive home from the meetinghouse that day was especially long and filled with unanswered questions. Had I counseled her correctly? Was I inspired? Did I help or hurt her hopes? Only time would bring answers to such questions.

* * *

Beauty for Ashes is a book about exchanges. Not the exchanges of physical objects, but rather our exchanges of self. By this I mean what we give or choose to do in response to what someone does or "gives" to us. These exchanges fill virtually every waking moment of our lives. They happen in our homes and with our neighbors. They occur as we drive to and from work and during much of our day in-between. They happen in our church meetings, at our family meals, at the grocery store—even when we're on vacation. In most instances the exchange is likely to be an uneven one, and in some situations, what someone gives is not something we wanted. Anger, jealousy, even violence. Or perhaps we're merely offered someone's indifference, sarcasm, or cutting and unkind words and actions. In a very literal way, these almost infinite human interactions and, more importantly, how we choose to respond to them, determine the quality of our mortal experience.

Learning how to control or to choose our responses to acts of spiritual or physical violence committed against us or against those we love is the central struggle of discipleship. The Lord Jesus Christ is our perfect model. As a scriptural summary of His mortal mission, the Savior used the following verses from Isaiah, a portion of which is quoted in the New Testament account found in Luke 4:16-22:

> The Spirit of the Lord God is upon me; because the Lord hath anointed me to preach good tidings unto the meek; he hath sent me to bind up the brokenhearted, to proclaim liberty to the captives, and the opening of the prison to them that are bound;
>
> To proclaim the acceptable year of the Lord, and the day of vengeance of our God; to comfort all that mourn;
>
> To appoint unto them that mourn in Zion, *to give unto them beauty for ashes*, the oil of joy for mourning, the garment of praise for the spirit of heaviness; that they might be called trees of righteousness, the planting of the Lord, that he might be glorified. (Isaiah 61:1–3; emphasis added)

To give . . . beauty for ashes. Isn't that the great test of our individual discipleship? Not only to give something beautiful when offered "ashes," but ultimately to become the Christlike response to the harsh, hurtful, and unfair things that are so much a part of mortal life. As the prophet Mormon put it in his exhortation to develop charity, we must acquire the pure love of Christ so "that when [the Savior] shall appear *we shall be like him*, for we shall see him as he is" (Moroni 7:48; emphasis added).

At the outset of our journey it is important to note what this book is not. It is not a how-to book. It is not a book outlining the five or twelve or whatever number of steps one can take to become Christlike in two weeks or less—guaranteed, or your money back. Our individual circumstances are far too varied to assume that a one-size-fits-all formula would exist. The process of becoming like the Savior is a lifetime, even eternal, experience. And it is an intensely personal work as well. Therefore, it is my hope that *Beauty for Ashes* will inspire you to believe that you can become the Christlike response to whatever hurt may come into your life. As such, the contents of the book are designed to be more compass than map, pointing you in the right direction without providing step-by-step instructions as to how to arrive at the ultimate objective: a Christlike life.

You may be wondering if things improved for this good sister who had lost all hope. Did her efforts to become more like the Savior in her responses to her husband have any effect on his heart? These are the questions we all ask when faced with the bitterness of a sometimes uncaring and unkind world. Can what I do and who I am really impact the lives of others? Will it really make a difference? How can I influence someone I love for good? Can who I am influence even my enemies or those that would do me harm? We need only look at the life of the Savior to find a clear and shining answer to such questions. More than two millennia later, we still treat His life as the perfect model for how we should be.

Choosing to focus on her own heart and inviting the Savior to change her responses not only affected this faithful but struggling sister's marriage, it changed her entire life. My heart was also changed as I watched her apply the Atonement in all of her relationships. As of the writing of this book, she is still married to this brother. Slowly, almost imperceptibly, his heart has begun to change. The powerful force of abiding love has proved too great for him to resist. He has watched as his wife has become more spiritually beautiful and has, after many years in the wilderness, begun to move toward the "promised land" her Christlike love has created for him.

I came to realize through this and many other experiences that there was much I did not understand about how Jesus Christ can change our hearts. Each chapter in *Beauty for Ashes* is the result of what I'm still learning along the way. My prayer is that it will help you to do as Alma encouraged in his great discourse on faith:

> Now as I said concerning faith—that it was not a perfect knowledge—even so it is with my words. Ye cannot know of their surety at first, unto perfection, any more than faith is a perfect knowledge.
>
> But behold, if ye will awake and arouse your faculties, even to an experiment upon my words, and exercise a particle of faith, yea, even if ye can no more than desire to believe, let this desire work in you, even until ye believe in a manner that ye can give place for a portion of my words.
>
> Now, we will compare the word unto a seed. Now, if ye give place, that a seed may be planted in your heart, behold, if it be a true seed, or a good seed, if ye do not cast it out by your unbelief, that ye will resist the Spirit of the Lord, behold, it will begin to swell within your breasts; and when you feel these swelling motions, ye will begin to say within yourselves-It must needs be that this is a good seed, or that the word is good, for it beginneth to enlarge my soul; yea, it beginneth to enlighten my understanding, yea, it beginneth to be delicious to me. (Alma 32:26–28)

Before proceeding further, it's important to further define my use of the word *ashes* throughout this book. To make it clear, the word *ashes*, for the purposes of this book, refers to the vast variety of obstacles and opposition we face in our day-to-day lives. These may be things as varied as a young child resisting our attempted correction, insensitivity from a neighbor or loved one, or the tragedy of emotional, sexual, or physical abuse.

Ashes to you might be the unfair treatment you receive from a coworker, a boss, or even a friend. It could include an innocent misunderstanding between you and a neighbor, or it may be deeply hurt feelings caused by a deliberate and malicious deception by a person you trusted. Simply put, any situation or interaction that requires us to choose the Christlike response could be labeled a "beauty for ashes" moment. Life seems almost overflowing with such "opportunities." We can respond to these circumstances with either "beauty" or "ashes." The Savior has shown and is still showing us the way. His way is beautiful.

CHAPTER 1

"Putteth off the natural man and becometh a saint through the atonement of Christ." —Mosiah 3:19

IT MUST HAVE BEEN QUIET that fateful night in the garden. At least in those first hours. The mob had not yet arrived. Except for Peter, James, and John, the rest of the Twelve Apostles were not in the Savior's immediate presence. The scriptural account indicates only that they were told to sit and wait while the Lord went farther to pray. With the exception of Judas Iscariot, we're not told what the disciples were doing during these dark hours. Sadly, we do know where Judas was and what he was doing. His motives aren't clear. Jealousy? Hurt feelings? Lack of understanding? Anger? Even if there were a recorded answer, it seems clear that it would do little to justify his traitorous actions, ironically sealed with a kiss on the cheek of the Innocent One. That awful act, and all that was to follow, were mere hours in the future. But first, as if betrayal, mockery, and Golgotha were not enough, there awaited the atoning agony of Gethsemane.

Matthew's account is the most detailed of the four Gospels regarding the events of that night. We're told that the Savior "began to be sorrowful and very heavy" (Matthew 26:37). He then told His three closest followers to "tarry ye here, and watch with me." Then "he went a little further, and fell on his face, and prayed, saying, O my Father, if it be possible, let this cup pass from me: nevertheless not as I will, but as thou wilt" (v. 39). Of the many lonely moments in His brief mortal sojourn, none had been as lonely and wrenching as this one. Gethsemane was the culmination of His mortal mission, the supernal act for which He had been so long preparing. Had He understood fully what it meant to say with perfect, selfless love, "Here am I, send me" (Abraham 3:27)? Elder Neal A. Maxwell shared this valuable insight as to this moment that "astonished" even Jesus:

> Imagine Jehovah, the Creator of this and other worlds, "astonished"! Jesus knew cognitively what He must do, but not experientially. He had never personally known the exquisite and exacting process of an atonement before. Thus, when the agony came in its fulness, it was so much, much worse than even He with his unique intellect had ever imagined! No wonder an angel appeared to strengthen him!
>
> The cumulative weight of all mortal sins—past, present, and future—pressed upon that perfect, sinless, and sensitive Soul! All our infirmities and sicknesses were somehow, too, a part of the awful arithmetic of the Atonement.
>
> The anguished Jesus not only pled with the Father that the hour and cup might pass from Him, but with this relevant citation. "And he said, Abba, Father, all things are possible unto thee; take away this cup from me." ("Willing to Submit," *Ensign*, April 1986)

Poignantly, upon returning to the three He had asked to watch and to pray for Him, He instead "findeth them asleep, and saith unto Peter, What, could ye not watch with me one hour?" (v. 40). This same scene was repeated twice. Each time He returned, no doubt hoping for comfort, for companionship, or even for mere acknowledgment of what He was suffering, but He instead found His three loyal but weary Apostles sleeping, "for their eyes were heavy."

At this moment in the recorded account, Joseph Smith inserts a mere nine words that tenderly amplify the significance of this experience. As part of his translation of the Bible, the Prophet added to verses 45 and 46 as follows: "Then cometh he to his disciples, and saith unto them, Sleep on now, and take your rest: behold, the hour is at hand, and the Son of man is betrayed into the hands of sinners. And after they had slept he said unto them, Rise, let us be going; behold, he is at hand that doth betray me." Those nine words, "and after they had slept he said unto them," provide an important insight into both the price and the power of a Christlike life.

Who needed the brief respite of sleep more than He? Which of the four men present most deserved succor, consolation, and relief? And yet, paradoxically, it was He that sat watching over Peter, James, and John as they slept. What pain must have wracked His body. What agony yet coursed through His pure and innocent soul. And yet, there in the soon-to-be-shattered quiet of the garden, the Atoning One stood watch over those He loved. The account is silent as to the length of time they slept. But this seemingly minor addition of these nine words into the story of that singular event teaches much about giving beauty for ashes.

The Savior was modeling, as He had always done, how to be as He is, regardless of circumstances. In sharing this it should not be implied that the disciples were unfeeling or selfish. They were tired. It was late in the evening, at the end of what had no doubt been a long and eventful day, even for them. And perhaps most importantly, they had at most a rudimentary understanding as to what their Master was even doing there in the garden. As far as they understood, He was simply praying and pondering, as He had often done, in a quiet place—a place the scriptures indicate He was accustomed or "wont" to retire to for prayer.

In offering himself as "an offering for sin," the Savior was providing all of His disciples with both the model and the means to become the Christlike response. His entire life was the model. And through His Atonement, He is able to change us through the gradual and at times arduous process of becoming "even as [He] is." As King Benjamin taught,

> For the natural man is an enemy to God, and has been from the fall of Adam, and will be, forever and ever, unless he yields to the enticings of the Holy Spirit, and putteth off the natural man, *and becometh a saint through the atonement of Christ the Lord*, and becometh as a child, submissive, meek, patient, full of love, willing to submit to all things which the Lord seeth fit to inflict upon him, even as a child doth submit to his father. (Mosiah 3:19; emphasis added)

Likewise, the Prophet Joseph Smith was taught in his sublime vision of the three degrees of glory that it is only through the Atonement of Jesus Christ that we are "made perfect": These are they who are just men *made perfect through Jesus the mediator of the new covenant*, who wrought out this perfect atonement through the shedding of his own blood (D&C 76:69; emphasis added).

These are lofty doctrines, difficult to fully comprehend. Often we may hear talks or lessons about the Atonement and think that it applies only to our hope of eternal life. Surely it can't apply to me, we think. To my problems, to my weaknesses, or to my struggles with my neighbor, a wayward child, or an obnoxious coworker or insensitive boss. Just the opposite is true. The virtue of the Atonement of Jesus Christ can change everything. It is not just for sinners. It applies to every problem, every weakness, and, most importantly, every relationship. When Joseph Smith cried out in sorrow and confusion to the Lord for relief during his dark hours in Liberty Jail, he was reminded, as we all need to be, that "The Son of Man hath descended below them all. Art thou greater than he?" (D&C 122:9). The Savior was not telling Joseph that his heartache wasn't real. Not at all. He was saying to Joseph, and to you and to me, I've been there, Joseph. There, with you, in Liberty Jail. I'll be there in Carthage, too. I was there when you and Emma lost those little babies. And in those moments when yet another mob smeared scalding tar on your body. I felt every hurt you felt. Received every blow and bruise you received. And I'm here—right now—to help you make it through. Because I was forsaken, you never, ever will be.

The Atonement of Jesus Christ can change anything. It is not just for sinners. It applies to every problem, every weakness, and every relationship.

Sister Cheiko Okazaki shared this profound insight regarding the relevance of the Atonement to our everyday, mortal probation:

The gospel is the good news that can free us from guilt. We know that Jesus experienced the totality of mortal existence in Gethsemane. It's our faith that he experienced everything—absolutely everything.

Sometimes we don't think through the implications of that belief. We talk in great generalities about the sins of all humankind, about the suffering of the entire human family. But we don't experience pain in generalities. We experience it individually. That means he knows what it felt like when your mother died of cancer—how it was for your mother, how it still is for you. He knows what it felt like to lose the student body election. He knows that moment when the brakes locked and the car started to skid. He experienced the slave ship sailing from Ghana toward Virginia. He experienced the gas chambers at Dachau. He experienced Napalm in Vietnam. He knows about drug addiction and alcoholism. Let me go further. There is nothing you have experienced . . . that he does not also know and recognize. On a profound level, he understands the hunger to hold your baby that sustains you through pregnancy. He understands both the physical pain of giving birth and the immense joy. He knows about PMS and cramps and menopause. He understands about rape and infertility and abortion. His last recorded words to his disciples were, "And, lo, I am with you always, even unto the end of the world." (Matthew 28:20).

He understands your mother-pain when your five-year-old leaves for kindergarten, when

> a bully picks on your fifth-grader, when your daughter calls to say that the new baby has Down syndrome. He knows your mother-rage when a trusted babysitter sexually abuses your two-year-old, when someone gives your thirteen-year-old drugs, when someone seduces your seventeen-year-old. He knows the pain you live with when you come home to a quiet apartment where the only children are visitors, when you hear that your former husband and his new wife were sealed in the temple last week, when your fiftieth wedding anniversary rolls around and your husband has been dead for two years. He knows all that. He's been there. He's been lower than all that. He's not waiting for us to be perfect. Perfect people don't need a Savior. He came to save his people in their imperfections. He is the Lord of the living, and the living make mistakes. He's not embarrassed by us, angry at us, or shocked. He wants us in our brokenness, in our unhappiness, in our guilt and our grief. (Cheiko Okazaki, *Lighten Up!* [Salt Lake City: Deseret Book, 1993], 174–175)

It's clear that we have much to learn about how the Savior can help us respond beautifully to the "ashes" we are given. His Atonement is both the model and the change agent for how, meaning that every moment of His brief mortal life showed us how to give beauty for ashes, and His Atonement makes becoming the Christlike response possible. Jesus is truly our perfect mentor. As the Apostle Paul taught, "For we have not an high priest which cannot be touched with the feeling of our infirmities; but was in all points tempted like as we are, yet without sin. Let us therefore come boldly to the throne of grace, that we may obtain mercy, and find grace to help in time of need" (Hebrews 4:15–16).

This passage suggests that the process of our becoming what and who it is that the Lord intends us to become is done at least in part through the grace of God. The concept of grace has a central role in the process of our becoming beauty for ashes in all of our personal exchanges. The grace of God is, as the Bible Dictionary teaches, an "enabling power," a power that enables "individuals, through faith in the atonement of Jesus Christ and the repentance of their sins, [to] receive strength and assistance to do good works that they otherwise would not be able to maintain if left to their own means" (LDS Bible Dictionary, 669).

Elder David A. Bednar offered important insights about the Savior's enabling grace in a talk he gave at Brigham Young University in October 2001:

> In Alma 7 we learn how and why the Savior is able to provide the enabling power, beginning with verse 11: "And he shall go forth, suffering *pains* and *afflictions* and *temptations* of every kind; and this that the word might be fulfilled which saith he will take upon him the *pains* and the *sicknesses* of his people" (emphasis added).
>
> Thus the Savior has suffered not just for our iniquities but also for the inequality, the unfairness, the pain, the anguish, and the emotional distress that so frequently beset us. Additional detail is described in verse 12:
>
> "And he will take upon him death, that he may loose the bands of death which bind his people; and he will take upon him their *infirmities*, that his bowels may be filled with mercy, according

> to the flesh, that he may know according to the flesh how to succor his people according to their infirmities" (emphasis added).
>
> There is no physical pain, no anguish of soul, no suffering of spirit, no infirmity or weakness that you or I ever experience during our mortal journey that the Savior did not experience first. You and I in a moment of weakness may cry out, "No one understands. No one knows." No human being, perhaps, knows. But the Son of God perfectly knows and understands, for He felt and bore our burdens before we ever did. And because He paid the ultimate price and bore that burden, He has perfect empathy and can extend to us His arm of mercy in so many phases of our life.
>
> He can reach out, touch, and succor—literally run to us—and strengthen us to be more than we could ever be and help us to do that which we could never do through relying only upon our own power. (David A. Bednar, "In the Strength of the Lord," *BYU Speeches*, 2001)

Our lives are filled with moments of feeling forsaken or of being mistreated, neglected, or even abused. Even those we love and trust have and will hurt us. For this reason, we begin to see why Mormon asked, "What is it that ye shall hope for?" His answer is the foundation for our work of becoming the Christlike response to our harsh and at times unfair mortal strifes: "Behold I say unto you that ye shall have hope through the atonement of Christ . . . and this because of your faith in him according to the promise" (Moroni 7:41).

As the Savior underwent the Atonement for our sins, our sicknesses, and our infirmities—"suffering pains and afflictions and temptations of every kind . . . that he [would] know according to the flesh how to succor his people according to their infirmities" (Alma 7:11, 13)—He acquired the divine empathy necessary to be "at one" with us in all of our experiences. In his sublime vision of the tree of life, Nephi was asked a question that we should all likewise ponder: "Knowest thou the condescension of God?" Perhaps we hear the word *condescension* and think of the word *condescending*. But this is a significant misunderstanding of what this word means and thus of how it applies to our present circumstances.

Through the Atonement, the Savior acquired the divine empathy necessary to be "at one" with us in all of our experiences.

The late Latter-day Saint scholar Eugene England elaborated on this in an essay he wrote about the Atonement and the writings of Shakespeare:

> The reason why only Christ can so affect us and how he does it are best made clear in the Book of Mormon. Very early in his translation of that ancient record, Joseph Smith uses a word that takes us right to the heart of the matter. Nephi, seeking confirmation of his father's spiritual experiences, is given a remarkable vision of the coming of Christ, still six hundred years in the future, in which Christ and his mission are

> referred to as "the condescension of God! . . . the Redeemer of the world" (1 Nephi 11:16, 26–27).
>
> The word chosen there is crucial: *condescension* has come to mean, in our time, treating a supposed inferior in false generosity. It corresponds to the word patronizing. But this is clearly not what the angel speaking to Nephi meant. Instead, that unusual term *condescension* was chosen to convey precisely the original meaning given by its Latin roots, *con* plus *descendere*, that is, "to descend with": Christ, as representing "the condescension of God," is the descending of God with us into all that we experience, including our sin and estrangement, and this is the heart of Christ's mission, the source of his unique power to achieve At One Ment. ("Shakespeare and the At One Ment of Jesus Christ," *Why the Church Is as True as the Gospel* [Salt Lake City: Bookcraft, 1986], 45–46)

An analogy that has helped me better understand how the Savior assists us through His Atonement may be useful here. In competitive bicycling, riders will sometimes attempt to "draft," or ride as closely as possible behind another rider, which significantly reduces the wind resistance caused when they race at very high speeds. This same idea can be likened to our efforts to become beauty for ashes.

As we draw closer to the Savior, He provides shelter from the turbulence of the world and leads us along the pathway of discipleship toward the finish line. He has experienced the course we're on from beginning to end. He knows every twist and turn, every steep uphill climb as well as every unseen danger along the way. Equally important, as we stay close to

Him throughout the race, we actually will become more and more like Him. We'll see as He sees, think as He thinks, and choose as He would choose. We can become "even as [He is]" (3 Nephi 27:27). This can be our experience, even when faced with the most awful evil imaginable.

Elder George F. Richards of the Quorum of the Twelve spoke about how daunting it can be to love our enemies and do good to those who hate us. Speaking in the general conference of October 1946, he shared an account of a dream he had had shortly before the end of World War II. The message of his dream is a sobering but significant one:

> I dreamed that I and a group of my own associates found ourselves in a courtyard where, around the outer edge of it, were German soldiers—and Fuhrer Adolph Hitler was there with his group, and they seemed to be sharpening their swords and cleaning their guns, and making preparations for a slaughter of some kind, or an execution. We knew not what, but, evidently we were the objects. But presently a circle was formed and this Fuhrer and his men were all within the circle, and my group and I were circled on the outside, and he was sitting on the inside of the circle with his back to the outside, and when we walked around and I got directly opposite to him, I stepped inside the circle and walked across to where he was sitting, and spoke to him in a manner something like this:
>
> "I am your brother. You are my brother. In our heavenly home we lived together in love and peace. Why can we not so live here on the earth?"

> And it seemed to me that I felt in myself, welling up in my soul, a love for that man, and I could feel that he was having the same experience, and presently he arose, and we embraced each other and kissed each other, a kiss of affection.
>
> Then the scene changed so that our group was within the circle, and he and his group were on the outside, and when he came around to where I was standing, he stepped inside the circle and embraced me again, with a kiss of affection.
>
> I think the Lord gave me that dream. Why should I dream of this man, one of the greatest enemies of mankind, and one of the wickedest, but that the Lord should teach me that I must love my enemies (Matt. 5:44), and I must love the wicked as well as the good?
>
> Now, who is there in this wide world that I could not love under those conditions, if I could only continue to feel as I felt then? I have tried to maintain this feeling and, thank the Lord, I have no enmity toward any person in this world; I can forgive all men, so far as I am concerned, and I am happy in doing so and in the love which I have for my fellow men." ("Love for Mankind," Conference Report, October 1946, 137–141)

This story is hard doctrine. To embrace and to kiss Adolf Hitler? To express love to one of the most evil and wicked men ever to walk the earth? A man responsible for the death of innocent millions? I readily confess being repelled by such a thought. And yet, the principles taught in this story are at the heart of the process of becoming beauty for ashes.

Through His Atonement, beginning in the Garden of Gethsemane and concluding on Calvary's cross, the Lord Jesus Christ has shown us the way and offers us assistance along the path to becoming "even as [He] is." His life and His suffering invite us into a fellowship with Him, a personal, customized curriculum that is built for our maximum spiritual development. In every instance in which we may face uncertainty as to what we should do, He stands close by, ready to provide "means unto . . . deliverance" (D&C 104:80). He knows exactly what we "lack yet," and has promised to provide compensating grace in helping us in overcoming our weakness. "And if men come unto me I will show unto them their weakness. I give unto men weakness that they may be humble; and my grace is sufficient for all men that humble themselves before me; for if they humble themselves before me, and have faith in me, then will I make weak things become strong unto them" (Ether 12:27).

His life and His suffering invite us into a fellowship with Him.

Jesus Christ is able to descend with us because He descended below us. And because he descended below us, He is able to assist and to enable us, through His grace, to "love our enemies, [to] bless them that curse you, [to] do good to them that hate you, and [to] pray for them which despitefully use you, and persecute you" (Matthew 5:44; 3 Nephi 12:44).

These principles of condescension and enabling grace relate directly to the process of becoming the Christlike response. The Savior came to earth to show us how and to help us to get back home to the presence of our Father in Heaven. Through

His Atonement, we obtain the virtue needed to respond as He would to our mortal heartaches and bruises. We obtain this virtue by asking for it in prayer, by learning about it through diligent study of the scriptures and the teachings of living prophets, and by seeking daily to apply the principles we learn. We develop further as Christlike disciples by worthily worshipping in holy temples, through serving humbly in callings and in our communities, and by striving to rise again when we fall short of what we know we should be (see D&C 117:13).

Inevitably, misunderstandings and mistreatment will come to each of us. The nature of what happens to us almost doesn't matter. How we choose to respond is the measure of our becoming beauty for ashes. Jesus Christ shows us the way.

CHAPTER 2

"Because of his loving kindness and long-suffering."
—1 Nephi 19:9

THE YOUNG PROPHET NEPHI PROVIDES us with a good example of someone who was given many opportunities to respond in a Christlike way to evil. Again and again his older brothers treated him unjustly. Again and again Nephi "frankly" forgave them, until it was clear that they were truly "past feeling."

At this point Nephi and his followers were directed to flee in order to preserve their lives. When Nephi wrote of the future coming of Jesus Christ, his heart must have been particularly tender when referring to how the Savior would respond to the cruel treatment He would receive at the hands of wicked men: "And the world, because of their iniquity, shall judge him to be a thing of naught; wherefore they scourge him and he suffereth it; and they smite him, and he suffereth it. Yea, they spit upon him and he suffereth it, *because of his loving kindness and his long-suffering* towards the children of men" (1 Nephi 19:9; emphasis added).

The Savior never allowed the way He was treated to determine how He would treat others. We must steadily and prayerfully strive to do likewise. Far easier said than done. When someone is unkind to us, our first impulse is almost always one of wanting justice. We feel justified in treating an offender in the same way he treated us, the Golden Rule notwithstanding. It's only fair, we think. Shouldn't we be allowed to do unto others as they did to us? Experiencing the "mighty change of heart" spoken of by Alma (see Alma 5:14) so that even our responses are motivated by love requires a force stronger than the feelings of anger or even hatred that may so easily beset us. But even before this power can be accessed and applied, our journey toward becoming the Christlike response begins with a choice.

In King Benjamin's sermon to his people, he mentions that we must become "willing to submit" (Mosiah 3:19; see also Alma 7:23, 13:28) in order to access the full transformative power of the Atonement. Having knowledge of what the Savior did for us is important but insufficient. We must also choose to live the disciple's life, especially when our discipleship is tested. Being kind and loving to others is far easier when we are being treated kindly. Reflexively choosing to give "beauty for ashes" is the divine standard for determining how far along we are in the process of becoming like the Savior.

This truth is illustrated in a story President Howard W. Hunter shared. As a young man, Vern Crowley learned the lesson taught by the Prophet Joseph Smith about loving others, even our enemies. When Vern's father became ill, fifteen-year-old Vern had to assume responsibility for running the family's wrecking yard. Sadly, some took advantage of the young man, and parts were being stolen from the yard. In his anger, Vern vowed to catch one of the thieves and make an example of him.

Sure enough, one night he caught a young thief stealing a transmission. His immediate impulse was to take the boy to the front office and call the police. But out of nowhere Vern's father appeared and asked to handle the situation. As President Hunter told it:

He then walked over to the young would-be thief and put his arm around his shoulder, looked him in the eye for a moment, and said, "Son, tell me, why are you doing this? Why were you trying to steal that transmission?" Then Mr. Crowley started walking toward the office with his arm around the boy, asking questions about the young man's car problems as they walked. By the time they had arrived at the office, the father said, "Well, I think your clutch is gone and that's causing your problem."

In the meantime, Vern was fuming. "Who cares about his clutch?" he thought. "Let's call the police and get this over with." But his father just kept talking. "Vern, get him a clutch. Get him a throwout bearing, too. And get him a pressure plate. That should take care of it." The father handed all of the parts to the young man who had attempted robbery and said, "Take these. And here's the transmission, too. You don't have to steal, young man. Just ask for it. There's a way out of every problem. People are willing to help."

Brother Vern Crowley said he learned an everlasting lesson in love that day. The young man came back to the lot often. Voluntarily, month by month, he paid for all of the parts Vic Crowley had given him, including the transmission. During those visits he asked Vern why his dad was the way he was and why he did what he did. Vern told him something of their Latter-day Saint beliefs and how much his father loved the Lord and loved people. Eventually the would-be thief was baptized. Vern later said, "It's hard now to describe the feelings I

> had and what I went through in that experience. I, too, was young. I had caught my crook. I was going to extract the utmost penalty. But my father taught me a different way. ("A More Excellent Way," *Ensign*, May 1992)

Brother Crowley's father clearly knew something about people that his son Vern did not yet know. He acted as if the crime committed against him didn't even happen. His focus was solely on applying mercy, not on exacting justice. We all aspire to be this way—to be kind when treated unkindly, to show love when we are hated, to be merciful to those who have been unjust in their dealings with us. But it can be so hard or even painful to do so. We have tender, fragile feelings. We want to be treated as a child of God should be treated, with respect, kindness, and with the "bonds of brotherly love." Sometimes we are the one being unkind or cruel, even though we claim to know better. Is it really possible to always be as we should be, regardless of what others may do to us? Could we do what Brother Crowley did if faced with similar circumstances? What must we do to always choose the right response? What must we do to become the right response?

Several years ago, newspaper columnist Sydney Harris shared the following experience he had with a Quaker friend in Chicago as they were buying a newspaper at a local newsstand:

> The Quaker bought a paper, then thanked the vendor politely. The vendor didn't so much as acknowledge his thanks.
>
> "Sullen fellow, isn't he?" Harris remarked.
>
> "I've been buying my papers from him for years, and he never responds," the Quaker quietly replied.
>
> "Why, then, do you continue to be polite to him?" Harris asked.

> The Quaker's answer was revealing. "Why should I let him determine how I act?" (Donald and Vesta Mansell, *Sure as the Dawn* [Review and Herald Publishing, July 1993]).

I love this little story and the lesson it teaches. Far too often I am guilty of allowing the way I am treated by others determine how I treat them. I have found that reminding myself of this Quaker gentleman's penetrating question—"Why should I let him determine how I act?"—has had a profound impact on how I choose to treat others. Is this true for you as well? Do you sometimes allow how you were treated by someone to influence how you feel about that person? Do you get stuck in giving ashes for ashes, even when your heart yearns to do otherwise?

We all fight this battle within. We know how we should act, and yet sometimes we do the opposite of what we know. Young Vern Crowley is a good example of this. He felt justified (and rightfully so) in wanting to exact a penalty from the young thief who was stealing car parts. Surely justice must be included in our dealings with others, yes? Evil must be opposed. But in what way? Paul teaches us, "Therefore if thine enemy hunger, feed him; if he thirst, give him drink: for in so doing thou shalt heap coals of fire on his head. Be not overcome of evil, but overcome evil with good" (Romans 12:21–22).

> Seeking only justice when we are wronged stunts our spiritual growth.

Seeking only justice when we are wronged stunts our spiritual growth and denies us the opportunity to assist someone else in his or her own efforts to experience the Savior's mercy. I like Paul's phrase, "Thou shalt heap coals of fire on his head." I take it that Paul is not encouraging me to start my enemies' heads on fire, but rather he's teaching me that by responding mercifully to those who may have offended me, I'm inviting the Savior to extend His mercy to those who have done me wrong. In so doing, both my enemy's and my hearts are transformed. As Joseph Smith taught, "Nothing is so much calculated to lead people to forsake sin as to take them by the hand, and watch over them with tenderness. When persons manifest the least kindness and love to me, O what power it has over my mind, while the opposite course has a tendency to harrow up all the harsh feelings and depress the human mind" (*History of the Church*, 5:23–24).

The good news is that we are not alone. The Savior can help us respond to opposition as He would when we exercise our agency and invite him to change our hearts.

> The good news is that we are not alone. The Savior can help us respond as He would.

This process is both ongoing and never-ending. And in the increasing strain of the latter days, it is more vital than ever before for us to "overcome evil with good."

Elder Robert D. Hales reminds us of this when he tells of a faithful sister who wondered why the Church doesn't more aggressively defend itself against accusations:

> To her inquiry I would say that one of mortality's great tests comes when our beliefs are questioned or criticized. In such moments, we may

> want to respond aggressively—to "put up our dukes." But these are important opportunities to step back, pray, and follow the Savior's example.
>
> Remember that Jesus Himself was despised and rejected by the world. . . . "The world hath hated [my disciples]," Jesus said, "because they are not of the world, even as I am not of the world" (John 17:14). [When] we respond to our accusers as the Savior did, we not only become more Christlike, we invite others to feel His love and follow Him as well. . . .
>
> Some people mistakenly think responses such as silence, meekness, forgiveness, and bearing humble testimony are passive or weak. But to "love [our] enemies, bless them that curse [us], do good to them that hate [us], and pray for them which despitefully use [us], and persecute [us]" (Matthew 5:44) takes faith, strength, and, most of all, Christian courage." ("The Price of Discipleship," *Ensign*, Nov. 2008)

Elder Hale'ss reminder that responding as the Savior would invites others to feel His love and follow Him as well is taught perfectly in the example of Vern Crowley's father. In responding with loving kindness to the young man's attempt to steal from him, Brother Crowley not only modeled giving "beauty for ashes," he also initiated the process of change within this young man's heart and his eventual decision to be baptized.

I'll talk more about this later, but I want to conclude this chapter with a story that powerfully captures the essence of giving "beauty for ashes," both for the one giving and the one receiving.

In a talk given at BYU, Brother C. Terry Warner shared this true story about a woman's relationship with her husband. The woman had suffered through her father's neglect, only to find that her husband was the same way. Whenever she asked why he was so distant, he said it was because she was always angry—which made her even more angry. She told him she was angry because he had withdrawn his love, which caused him to withdraw even more. In a burst of frustration, she decided to write down all her grievances so her husband could understand how she felt. But as she was writing, a peculiar thing happened to her: the more she wrote, the more she felt that what she was writing was false. And she felt that the feeling came from God.

> So I tore up the pages I had written, threw myself down on my knees, and began to pray, saying, "If it is false, show me how it could be false." And then a voice spoke to my mind and said, "If you had come unto Me, it all would have been different." I was astounded. . . . [I]nto my mind flashed pictures of me wanting to do things my own way, of holding grudges, of not forgiving, of not loving as God had loved us. I had wanted my husband to "pay" for my emotional suffering. I had not let go of the past and had not loved God with all my heart. I loved my own willful self more. I was aghast. I suddenly realized that I was responsible for my own suffering, for if I had really come unto Him, as I outwardly thought I had done, it all would have been different. As that horrible truth settled over me, I realized why the pages I had written of my suffering had been false. I had allowed it to happen by not truly coming unto God. That day I repented of not loving God, of not loving my husband, of blaming, of finding fault, of thinking that others were responsible for my misery.

> . . . I tried to come unto God with full purpose of heart. I prayed more earnestly and listened to His Spirit. I read my scriptures and tried to come to know Him better. Two months passed, and one morning my husband awoke and turned to me in bed and said, "You know, we find fault too much with each other. I am never going to find fault with my wife again." I was flabbergasted, for he had never admitted he had done anything wrong in our relationship. He did stop finding fault, and he began to compliment me and show sweet kindness. It was as if an icy glass wall between us had melted away. Almost overnight our relationship became warm and sweet. Three years have passed, and still it continues warmer and happier. We care deeply about one another and share ideas and thoughts and feelings, something we had not done for the first 16 years of marriage. (C. Terry Warner, "Honest, Simple, Solid, True," *BYU Speeches*, Jan. 16, 1996)

If you had come unto Me, it all would have been different. That is for me the perfect summation of how transformational the power of striving to become "beauty for ashes" can ultimately be. By first coming unto Christ, working to diligently strengthen our understanding and application of His Atonement, we can then become the Christlike response to those we once called our enemies. And in turn we can choose to love them unconditionally, even if they choose not to change as we believe they should. It is as the Lord reminded Hyrum Smith on the morning before he and his brother Joseph were martyred at Carthage, as recounted in John Taylor's record of the events:

> When Joseph went to Carthage to deliver himself up to the pretended requirements of the law, two or three days previous to his assassination, he said: "I am going like a lamb to the slaughter; but I am calm as a summer's morning; I have a conscience void of offense towards God, and towards all men. I shall die innocent, and it shall yet be said of me—he was murdered in cold blood."—The same morning, after Hyrum had made ready to go—shall it be said to the slaughter? Yes, for so it was—he read the following paragraph, near the close of the twelfth chapter of Ether, in the Book of Mormon, and turned down the leaf upon it:
>
> *And it came to pass that I prayed unto the Lord that he would give unto the Gentiles grace, that they might have charity. And it came to pass that the Lord said unto me: If they have not charity it mattereth not unto thee, thou hast been faithful; wherefore thy garments shall be made clean.* (D&C 135:4–5)

We cannot ultimately change another person's heart, although we can certainly help facilitate that process through our responses to that person. But as Hyrum read in the book of Ether, when it is between us and the Savior, "It mattereth not unto thee, thou hast been faithful" are the sweetest words He might ever speak to a bruised but resolute believer.

CHAPTER 3

"Love your enemies." —Matthew 5:44

In the Savior's description of the world during the thousand-year Millennium, He teaches us that this remarkable time will include the end of enmity: "And in that day the enmity of man, and the enmity of beasts, yea, the enmity of all flesh, shall cease from before my face" (D&C 101:26). What is enmity? The dictionary defines it as "the state or feeling of being actively opposed or hostile to someone or something." Our first introduction to the idea of enmity comes from the account of Adam and Eve in the Garden of Eden. After they were tempted by Satan to eat of the fruit of the tree of the knowledge of good and evil, God tells the devil that he "will put enmity between thee and the woman, and between thy seed and her seed; it shall bruise thy head, and thou shalt bruise his heel" (Genesis 3:15).

From that day to the present, Satan and his followers have been "actively hostile" against the Savior and His followers. The war they are waging is intended to encourage us to mimic their hostility. "For verily, verily, I say unto you, he that hath the spirit of contention is not of me, but is of the devil, who is the father of contention, and he stirreth up the hearts of men to contend with anger, one with another" (3 Nephi 11:29). We are up against stiff opposition. They are ceaseless in their assaults. The harder we strive, the more intense their efforts become.

In his stirring warning to beware of pride, President Ezra Taft Benson included enmity as a central component of this universal sin:

> Most of us think of pride as self-centeredness, conceit, boastfulness, arrogance, or haughtiness. All of these are elements of the sin, but the heart, or core, is still missing.
>
> The central feature of pride is enmity—enmity toward God and enmity toward our fellowmen. Enmity means "hatred toward, hostility to, or a state of opposition." It is the power by which Satan wishes to reign over us. ("Beware of Pride," *Ensign*, April 1989)

As the scriptures and prophets both make clear, enmity is a state we must work diligently to avoid. And yet our lives are filled with moments in which we are at enmity with someone. It could be a neighbor who treated one of our children unkindly or a ward member who criticizes the way we taught a class or handled a meeting. It may often include those closest to us—our spouse, children, or another family member. Sometimes the offense is intentional, but more often it is not. We all say things we probably shouldn't say. We all make choices that can cause hurt or misunderstanding with someone we love. Much of the tapestry of life is woven with threads that we would not have chosen to include in our tapestry. If there is enmity between us and someone we know, whether instigated by them or by us, it behooves us to seek for a way to become "repairers of the breach" (Isaiah 58:12) that divides us.

The Sermon on the Mount follows an interesting pattern. The Savior begins with the soothing, gentle words of beatitude. "Blessed" is the state promised again and again to those who choose the disciple's path. He then teaches the importance of being "the light of the world" and of the importance of avoiding hypocrisy. But then the tone begins to shift. Jesus teaches us that if there is cause for disagreement between us and a brother, that we must "first be reconciled to thy brother" before offering a sacrifice or gift at the altar. The Savior counsels us to "agree with thine adversary quickly, while thou art in the way with him" (Matthew 5:25). Then the waters of discipleship become even more brisk:

> Ye have heard that it hath been said, An eye for an eye, and a tooth for a tooth:
>
> But I say unto you, That ye resist not evil: but whosoever shall smite thee on thy right cheek, turn to him the other also.
>
> And if any man will sue thee at the law, and take away thy coat, let him have thy cloak also.
>
> And whosoever shall compel thee to go a mile, go with him twain.
>
> Give to him that asketh thee, and from him that would borrow of thee turn not thou away. (Matthew 5:38–42)

Shifting from "blessed are the meek: for they shall inherit the earth" to "turn to him the other [cheek] also" seems an abrupt and unfair transition. Doesn't following Christ qualify us for some type of exemption from suffering or opposition? Shouldn't we be shielded from the consequences of the wickedness or insensitivity of others? But there's more.

Just before He exhorts us to be perfect, "even as [our] Father which is in heaven is perfect," the Savior teaches perhaps the most wintry of His divine doctrines as prerequisite to our becoming "the children of [our] Father which is in heaven":

> Ye have heard that it hath been said, Thou shalt love thy neighbour, and hate thine enemy.
>
> But I say unto you, Love your enemies, bless them that curse you, do good to them that hate you, and pray for them which despitefully use you, and persecute you. (Matthew 5:43–44)

Really? Love our enemies? Bless them that curse us? Do good to them that hate us? And pray for those who despitefully use or even persecute us? Sister Mary Ellen Edmunds gave the following in answer to the question "How is it possible to have charity for all people, including our enemies?":

> The Savior said his disciples would be known by their love for each other and by their treatment of their enemies (see John 13:34–35; Matt. 5:44).
>
> President Brigham Young exemplified the attitude and actions that reflect a truly Christ-like love—kind, charitable feelings that extend beyond our families and friends to include even our adversaries: "I feel at peace with all the inhabitants of the earth; I love my friends, and as for my enemies, I pray for them daily; and, if they do not believe I would do them good, let them call at my house, when they are hungry, and I will feed them; yea, I will do good to those who despitefully use and persecute me" (*Discourses of Brigham Young,* sel. John A. Widtsoe [Salt Lake City: Deseret Book Co., 1978], 457).
>
> 'Why does the Lord ask you to love your enemies and to return good for evil? That *you*

> might have the benefit of it. It does not injure him [your enemy] so much when you hate a person, especially if he is far removed and does not come in contact with you, but the hate and the bitterness canker your unforgiving heart," said President Kimball (*The Teachings of Spencer W. Kimball,* p. 103). ("I Have a Question," *Ensign*, Dec. 1995, 12)

One of the most remarkable stories in the Book of Mormon is one that may be easily overlooked. It is the account in Alma 24 about the people who were known as the Anti-Nephi-Lehies. It is especially relevant when applied to the idea of overcoming enmity toward our "enemies." The Anti-Nephi-Lehies were a group of converts taught by Ammon and his fellow missionaries. As the story begins, the king of the Lamanites and those who were miraculously converted "were desirous that they might have a name, that thereby they might be distinguished from their brethren, the Lamanites. Before the king died, he even changed his son's name to Anti-Nephi-Lehi as he conferred the kingdom upon him. But not everyone was pleased with this.

A group of estranged Nephites, now known as the Amalekites and Amulonites, were so angered by their king's actions that "their hatred became exceedingly sore against them, even insomuch that they began to rebel against their king . . . therefore they took up arms against the people of Anti-Nephi-Lehi." Great violence was about to erupt within the Lamanite kingdom. Ammon and his brethren "saw the preparations of the Lamanites to destroy their brethren" and felt compelled to save the lives of those they had already helped to save spiritually. They gathered in the land of Ishmael "that they might hold a council with Lamoni and also with his brother Anti-Nephi-Lehi, what they should do to defend themselves against the Lamanites."

Part of their difficulty came as the result of the Anti-Nephi-Lehies' total refusal to defend themselves. "Now there was not one soul among all the people who been converted unto the Lord that would take up arms against their brethren; nay, *they would even make any preparations for war*; yea, and also their king commanded them that they should not" (Alma 24:6; emphasis added). The account includes the words of this courageous young king, recounting for his people the necessity of their giving "beauty for ashes" to the Lamanites, even if it would cost them their lives. He reminds them that God had granted that they "might repent of these things, and also that he hath forgiven us of those our many sins and murders which we have committed, and taken away the guilt from our hearts, through the merits of his Son" (v. 10).

Then, to affirm with action what they had expressed in word, "all the people . . . assembled together . . . took their swords, and all the weapons that were used for the shedding of man's blood, and they did bury them up deep in the earth. And this they did, it being in their view a testimony to God, and also to men, that they never would use weapons again for the shedding of man's blood; and this they did, vouching and covenanting with God, that rather than shed the blood of their brethren they would give up their own lives; and rather than spend their days in idleness they would labor abundantly with their hands" (Alma 24:18). Knowing that the Anti-Nephi-Lehies had entered into this covenant and having witnessed them burying their "weapons of war, for peace," Ammon and his brethren were no doubt desperate to protect them. But it was not to be.

As the Lamanites approached, fully armed, with the intent "of destroying the king, and to place another in his stead, and also of destroying the people of Anti-Nephi-Lehi out of the land," the hearts of the Nephite missionaries must have been near to breaking as they watched what then occurred. "Now when the [Anti-Nephi-Lehies] saw that [the Lamanites] were coming against them *they went out to meet them*, and prostrated themselves before them on the earth, and began to call upon the name of the Lord; *and thus they were in this attitude* when the Lamanites began to fall upon them, and began to slay them with the sword. And thus *without meeting any resistance*, they did slay a thousand and five of them" (Alma 24:21–22; emphasis added).

Can you imagine what this scene must have looked like? To watch men, women, and children lying down at the feet of their enemies, praising God at the very moment that He allowed them to be slain? Is there a more dramatic example in all of scripture of anyone "loving their enemies . . . doing good to them that hate you" or "praying for them that despitefully use you and persecute you"? As Mormon reminds us in his recounting of the story, "And thus we see that, when these Lamanites were brought to believe and to know the truth, they were firm, and would rather suffer even unto death rather than commit sin; and thus we see that they buried their weapons of peace, or rather, that they buried their weapons of war, for peace" (Alma 24:19).

As the Lamanites realized that their violence was not being met with violence but rather with abject humility, the full power of the Anti-Nephi-Lehies' conversion began to sink into their enemies' hearts. "Now when the Lamanites saw this they did forbear from slaying them; and there were many whose hearts had swollen in them for those of their brethren who had fallen under the sword, for they had repented of the things which they had done" (Alma 24:24). The profound power of becoming "beauty for ashes" as it relates to changing another person's heart is reflected in the conclusion to this account: "And it came to pass that [the Lamanites] threw down their weapons of war, and they would not take them again, *for they were stung for the murders which they had committed*; and they came down even as their brethren, relying upon the mercies of those whose arms were lifted to slay them" (Alma 24:25; emphasis added).

Clearly this story was included in the pages of the Book of Mormon as a lesson to latter-day readers. When we are committed to being "even as [He] is," regardless of what such a commitment might cost us, the power of that act cannot be restrained from influencing those around us, even those who might have once been called our "enemies." As the story of the Anti-Nephi-Lehies reminds us, laying down our "weapons of war," even to the extent of burying them deep in the earth, does not mean that others will instantly cease their hostilities against us. Those who would do us harm or even simply those who have hurt us unintentionally may never change or acknowledge their offense. In some cases, our unwillingness to "take up arms" may in fact cause their anger to increase. We cannot directly control another person's choices. Such control was the central theme of Lucifer's failed attempt to destroy the Father's plan of happiness (see Moses 4:1–4).

The invitation from the Savior to "love our enemies" was taught with full knowledge of what it might cost us to do so.

The invitation from the Savior to "love our enemies" was taught with full knowledge of what it might cost us to do so. Who better than He who cried in the midst of fully undeserved agony from the cross—"Father forgive them, for they know not what they do"—to model for His disciples that such love can be very costly? And yet, if we are to be known as His, we must love our enemies even as He did and does. Of course, our suffering or hurt can never be compared, at least equally, to the awful suffering experienced by Jesus Christ on our behalf. But in our day-to-day experiences and interactions, we have limitless opportunities to reflect His "image in [our] countenances" (Alma 5:14). And the hearts of others, unbeknownst to us, may also be changed because of our striving to become "beauty for ashes."

An LDS sister recounted an experience she had in which she learned, somewhat begrudgingly, the power of loving those who despitefully or unkindly use us. Her family had moved into an apartment complex and discovered their outdoor faucet didn't work. When she asked the woman living next door if they might use her faucet, she was bluntly told no and to not bother her again. Soon after the woman moved to another apartment at the far end of the complex, and with some relief this sister thought her troubles with this neighbor had ended.

But after being encouraged in a Sunday School class to "love her enemies," she realized she needed to at least make an attempt to give "beauty for ashes" to this woman. Each day she would hang out her laundry on the clothesline that sat next to the woman's apartment. She would often sit outside alone, smoking and drinking coffee. The sister said "hello" to the woman and was ignored. This was repeated several more times over a period of weeks, and each time the woman merely glared at her. And then something changed.

> One morning, after about two weeks, much to my surprise, she walked over to where I was hanging wet clothes and exchanged a few remarks about the weather.
>
> After that, each day when I came to hang out clothes, she came over and we said a few words—never anything personal . . . I certainly never felt that we were friends in any sense of the word. She always seemed cold and reserved in her attitude.

> Then one day my husband and I received word that we were to be transferred to a different locality. When I went out the next morning to hang my washing, the woman came to the clothesline as usual to talk. I told her that we were moving away.
>
> About an hour after I had gone home, the woman appeared at my door. . . . Neither of us had ever been in the other's apartment. She had an odd, strained expression on her face. I invited her to sit down and we tried to talk a little. But there really seemed to be nothing to talk about.
>
> Then, to my astonishment, she burst into tears, sobbing as if her heart would break. She said she couldn't stand to have me move away. "You are the only friend I have in the whole world," she said.
>
> Me! Why, I didn't even know her first name!
>
> I couldn't think of anything to say to my friend. I only knew that we weren't enemies any more.
>
> "Oh, Father," I thought. "Forgive me for doubting your word. I didn't really do anything for her. I only said hello and visited with her a little. What a flood of proof you've given me!" (Rena Evers, "Proving the Principle of Loving Your Enemies," *Liahona*, Dec. 1984, 23–24)

Can the hearts of our "enemies" be changed through us? Without question. As the story of the Anti-Nephi-Lehies makes clear, loving and doing good to our enemies can bring about profound, even miraculous changes in their hearts. And if we are to live in a millennial state where "the enmity of all flesh . . . shall cease," then clearly we must learn to love others without condition or exception.

CHAPTER 4

"No more disposition to do evil, but to do good continually."
—Mosiah 5:2

THERE IS A SUBTLE BUT important difference between our responding to mistreatment or unkindness in a Christlike way and our actually becoming like the Savior. In fact, both responding and becoming are important parts of the process, each necessary to our mortal experience. Responding and becoming are sequential. We can't skip steps or take shortcuts in going through the process of having our hearts divinely altered. As Elder Richard G. Scott has taught, "We become what we want to be by consistently being what we want to become each day" (Richard G. Scott, "The Transforming Power of Faith and Character," *Ensign*, Nov. 2010, 43–46). In other words, if we want to become the Christlike response to everyone and everything, we must first strive each day to be more like the Savior, even when doing so is contrary to our instincts or impulses.

The story of Joseph of Egypt is illustrative in this regard. Joseph was truly an innocent victim of heartbreaking violence against him. Even worse, it was caused by those he loved and trusted: his older brothers. The basic outline of the story is familiar.

Seventeen-year-old Joseph was sent by his father, Jacob, to check on the flocks his brothers were tending. This was preceded by Joseph's having two distinct dreams, both of which implied that his older brothers and even his father would make "obeisance" to him. When he shared these accounts with his brothers, they "hated" and "envied him." With the cankering seeds of enmity firmly rooted in their hearts, it is still shocking to read that "when they saw [Joseph] afar off, even before he came near unto them, they conspired against him to slay him" (Genesis 37:18).

Joseph's brother Rueben steps in to prevent Joseph from being murdered, but his suggested alternative is certainly not much better: "Shed no blood, but cast him into this pit that is in the wilderness, and lay no hand upon him . . . and it came to pass, when Joseph was come unto his brethren, that they stript Joseph out of his coat, his coat of many colours that was on him; And they took him, and cast him into the pit: and the pit was empty, there was no water in it" (Genesis 37:22–24).

Can you imagine how Joseph must have been feeling? Here he was, coming by assignment to make sure that his brothers were doing well (no doubt carrying provisions with him), and instead of being welcomed by them, he is stripped of his coat—the gift given to him as a sign of favor by Jacob—and then thrown angrily into a pit. Things then go from hurtful to horrible for Joseph. As his "brethren" sit down to eat bread, they see a company of Ishmeelites approaching on their way to sell spices in Egypt. Judah callously suggests that rather than slay Joseph they should instead sell him to the approaching Ishmeelites, "for he is our brother and our flesh."

Joseph is then pulled unceremoniously from the pit he'd just been thrown into and sold to the Ishmeelites "for twenty pieces of silver" (a foreshadowing perhaps of another Innocent One being betrayed by someone He loved and trusted?). I can't imagine that any of Joseph's brothers could even look him in the eye at this moment. And how must he have felt about them? Surely he was heartbroken, confused, and angry. Rightfully so. His brothers' treatment of him was inexcusable and a direct and grievous violation of both Hebrew and divine law.

The scriptures are silent as to what might have been said or unsaid between them. Joseph was taken as a slave to Egypt. His brothers then returned home with cruel lies to tell. After staining Joseph's coat with goat's blood, they went to Jacob and told him they'd found the coat and wondered if it might be Joseph's. Jacob's heart was broken. His innocent son Joseph had been slain by a wild beast. "And all his sons and all his daughters rose up to comfort him; but he refused to be comforted" (Genesis 37:35). The callousness of his older sons is stunning.

> We need to drink the bitter cup without becoming bitter.

Meanwhile, young Joseph, as he would show throughout this experience, trusted in God's love for him. Even though it would have been both easy and understandable for Joseph to harbor bitterness for what had unfairly happened to him, he understood the importance of what Elder Neal A. Maxwell taught—that we "drink the bitter cup without becoming bitter." Joseph became the servant of Potiphar, an officer of Pharaoh, and after observing that "the Lord was with [Joseph]," Potiphar made Joseph the overseer over all of his household. Things were looking up for Joseph. After the stunning injustice he'd suffered at the hands of his brethren, heaven was smiling on him again. New opportunities, ones that he likely would not have been given had he remained in Canaan with his family, were being given him. Life was good. "And Joseph was a goodly person, and well favoured" (Genesis 39:3).

It was then that Joseph's test was expanded. Potiphar's wife began to lust after this vibrant young man and demanded that he "lie with [her]." *Why me?* Joseph may have wondered. Just when everything was looking up, yet another test! Joseph resisted. Potiphar's wife persisted. Joseph attempted to reason with her. After reminding her that Potiphar had committed everything but his wife into Joseph's care, he pleaded, "How then can I do this great wickedness, and sin against God?" (Genesis 39:9). But she wouldn't relent. Again and again, day after day, she tried to seduce Joseph. Again and again he resisted. Then at last the opportunity she'd been hoping for arrived. Alone in the house, she cornered Joseph and demanded that he give in to her evil demands. But Joseph "left his garment in her hand, and got him out."

The outcome is well known. Joseph was falsely accused by Potiphar's wife and was thrown into prison. Again, as with his brethren in the wilderness, Joseph was innocent. He had done nothing wrong. In fact, he had resisted evil in spite of a relentless attempt by Potiphar's wife to cause him to yield to the "natural man." And what did he get in exchange for his obedience? More injustice. More unfair treatment. More ashes.

Surely now Joseph deserved to complain. Surely now he could shake his fist at heaven and demand that he be given justice. Although the account does not say so explicitly, it seems clear from Joseph's responses to evil and unfair treatment that he retained his faith in God's ability to make everything right. "But the Lord was with Joseph, and shewed him mercy, and gave him favour in the sight of the keeper of the prison" (Genesis 39:21).

As before, with the help of heaven, Joseph again made the best of a bad situation. He was soon given responsibility over all of the prisoners in the prison "because the Lord was with him" (Genesis 39:23). It is significant to me that Joseph was able to obtain such a remarkable blessing through quiet, consistent obedience.

As it was for Joseph, so it can be for each of us. Nowhere in the scriptures are we promised freedom from adversity or opposition. Bad days (or weeks or years) come to all of us. We are here to be proven, after all. And that proving is custom-built for each of us by the hands of the Master Builder. Joseph clearly had personal clarity in his understanding of his relationship to God. Although much of his story is colored with hard moments, he never appears to become hardened by those moments. The "ashes" that repeatedly came his way appeared only to make Joseph's soul more "beautiful," more divine, and more Christlike.

The story continued with the incarceration of the royal butler and baker in the prison. Both were sent there because they'd offended Pharaoh. Sometime after arriving in prison, both men had a dream on the same night and awoke in sorrow because "there [was] no interpreter of it." Joseph reminded them that God had given him the ability to interpret dreams, which interpretation he then provided for each of them. The butler's dream had a happy ending, with him being restored to his former position in Pharaoh's court. The baker's story ended much differently, and it's likely he regretted allowing Joseph to interpret his dream. Joseph pled with the chief butler to remember his cause before the king upon his release, "yet did not the chief butler remember Joseph, but forgat him" (Genesis 40:23).

Two years passed. As far as the record indicates, Joseph continued to be Joseph, ever faithful and submissive. Then Pharaoh had a dream about the seven fat and seven lean kine, or cattle. This was followed by a similar dream about seven ears of healthy and seven ears of thin ("blasted") corn. Pharaoh was troubled by this and sought for someone in his court to interpret these dreams. At last remembering the young man who had interpreted his dream in prison, the butler told Pharaoh about him. Joseph was brought before the king and correctly interpreted his dreams. At last his moment had come. "And Pharaoh said unto Joseph, Forasmuch as God hath showed thee all this, there is none so discreet and wise as thou art: Thou shalt be over my house, and according unto thy word shall all my people be ruled: only in the throne will I be greater than thou. And Pharaoh took off his ring from his hand, and put it on Joseph's hand, and arrayed him in vestures of fine linen, and put a gold chain about his neck . . . and he made him ruler over all the land of Egypt" (Genesis 40:40–43).

Joseph was thirty years old when he was made Egypt's ruler. He was seventeen when his brothers threw him into a pit. For thirteen years he was either a servant or a prisoner. Throughout these trials he remained steady and submissive, "willing to submit to all things which the Lord [saw] fit to inflict upon him, even as a child doth submit to his father" (Mosiah 3:19). Because he trusted in the Lord in spite of all apparent indications that he'd been forgotten, heaven made things right, as heaven always does.

As President Gordon B. Hinckley once said, "It isn't as bad as you sometimes think it is. It all works out. Don't worry. I say that to myself every morning. It will all work out. If you do your best, it will all work out. Put your trust in God, and move forward with faith and confidence in the future. The Lord will not forsake us. He will not forsake us. . . . If we will put our trust in Him, if we will pray to Him, if we will live worthy of His blessings, He will hear our prayers" (Jordan Utah South Regional Conference, Priesthood Session, 1 March 1997).

Then Joseph's moment to obtain justice finally arrived. At the end of the seven "fat" years, the famine foreseen in the Pharaoh's dreams began. Joseph's father, Jacob, sent his sons to Egypt because he had heard that there was food made available for his family. All but Benjamin, Jacob's youngest, headed to Egypt. Joseph was now governor over the land and the one responsible for distributing all of the food stores. When his ten brothers arrived, Joseph immediately knew who they were, "but they knew not him." Twenty years had passed since that terrible moment when he had been cast into a pit, after which he'd been treated as their property and sold to some traveling merchants. Now the tables were turned. Now was Joseph's opportunity for fully justified payback.

I pause at this point in the story to reflect on what I would do if I were in Joseph's position. With the authority he held, he likely could have had all ten of his brothers cast into prison, and he would have been considered "right." Without knowing the intricacies of Egyptian law, I assume it's possible that he could have even had them put to death. But Joseph chose another path, the "beauty for ashes" way.

After asking his brethren where they had come from, he accused them of being spies. It seems clear that he was being neither spiteful nor cruel, but was in essence helping his older brothers begin to repent. After learning that there was yet another son—Benjamin, who was not present—Joseph told them that unless the youngest was brought to him, he would not allow the ten brothers to return home. And to ensure that they would make good, he required that they leave one of their company, Simeon, behind as a form of collateral.

Although it had been two decades since their inhumane act, the pangs of guilt and remorse over their brutal treatment of Joseph still lingered in their hearts. "And they said one to another, We are verily guilty concerning our brother, in that we saw the anguish of his soul, when he besought us, and we would not hear; therefore is this distress come upon us" (Genesis 42:21). Reuben reminded them that he had warned them over sinning against Joseph but they wouldn't listen. Throughout their discussion they were unaware that Joseph could understand every word, as he had been speaking to them through an interpreter. His character is revealed yet again, and poignantly so. "And he turned himself from them, and wept; and returned to them again, and communed with them, and took from them Simeon, and bound him before their eyes" (Genesis 42:24).

Joseph then commanded his servants to include all of the money that his brothers had brought for payment in the sacks of grain with which he had sent them home. This wasn't discovered until they stopped to feed their animals. "And their heart failed them, and they were afraid, saying one to another, What is this that God hath done unto us?" (Genesis 42:28). Upon returning home, they recounted to Jacob their tale of woe and then conveyed Joseph's demand that Benjamin be brought to him. They also shared with their father the fact that the money they'd given for food had been sent back with them. There is a beautiful metaphor in this act of grace by Joseph. It teaches something about how our Father in Heaven extends His mercy to us in spite of our unworthiness to receive it. Joseph's brothers had done nothing to "deserve" his forgiveness. And yet, by sending them home with both the needed grain and the money they'd used to purchase it, he teaches us how to give "beauty for ashes." Joseph's response was the Christlike response.

Luke records the Savior's instructions from the Sermon on the Mount differently than does Matthew. I find his additions to the account significant:

> But I say unto you which hear, Love your enemies, do good to them which hate you, Bless them that curse you, and pray for them which despitefully use you.
>
> And unto him that smiteth thee on the one cheek offer also the other; and him that taketh away thy cloak forbid not to take thy coat also. Give to every man that asketh of thee; and of him that taketh away thy goods ask them not again.
>
> And as ye would that men should do to you, do ye also to them likewise. For if ye love them which love you, what thank have ye? For

> sinners also love those that love them. And if ye do good to them which do good to you, what thank have ye? for sinners also do even the same. And if ye lend to them of whom ye hope to receive, what thank have ye? for sinners also lend to sinners, to receive as much again.
>
> But love ye your enemies, and do good, and lend, hoping for nothing again; and your reward shall be great, and ye shall be the children of the Highest: for he is kind unto the unthankful and to the evil. Be ye therefore merciful, as your Father also is merciful. Judge not, and ye shall not be judged: condemn not, and ye shall not be condemned: forgive, and ye shall be forgiven:
>
> Give, and it shall be given unto you; good measure, pressed down, and shaken together, and running over, shall men give into your bosom. For with the same measure that ye mete withal it shall be measured to you again. (Luke 6:27–38)

I especially love that last verse and its reminder to me of how heaven blesses us "notwithstanding [our] weakness" (2 Nephi 33:11). "Give, and it shall be given to you; good measure, pressed down, and shaken together, and running over, shall men give unto your bosom. For with the same measure that ye mete withal it shall be measured to you again." As President J. Reuben Clark taught, "I believe that in His justice and mercy [God] will give us the maximum reward for our acts, give us all that he can give, and in the reverse, I believe that he will impose upon us the minimum penalty which it is possible for him to impose" (Conference Report, Sept. 30, 1955, 24). Joseph was acting in a similar manner here. He was trying in every way possible to convey both love and forgiveness to his brothers.

At first Jacob resists sending Benjamin back to Egypt, even though it means that he is now missing another son, Simeon, who has been detained by Joseph. But the realities of their diminishing food supplies at last persuade him, although reluctantly, that the only way to feed his family and to have Simeon restored to him is to send Benjamin back to Egypt with his remaining sons.

Upon their arrival, the brothers go to Joseph's house, fearful of what may happen. Perhaps he will accuse them of stealing from him and have all of them cast into prison. Perhaps he will require all of their property. They quickly seek out Joseph's steward and relate to him the apparent error that occurred during their previous journey. The steward assures them that they have nothing to fear and then brings Simeon out to them. He then takes them to Joseph's house, where they are allowed to bathe and to care for their animals. Joseph then arrives again on the scene.

After asking about their father's welfare, he "saw his brother Benjamin, his mother's son, and said, Is this your younger brother, of whom ye spake unto me? And he said, God be gracious unto thee, my son. And Joseph made haste; for his bowels did yearn upon his brother: and he sought where to weep; and he entered into his chamber, and wept there" (Genesis 43:29–30).

After regaining his composure, Joseph then arranges for his brothers to eat. They are astonished at this treatment, including the fact that Joseph sends five times as much food to Benjamin as he does to the rest of them. Again, it doesn't appear that he is attempting to be spiteful or vengeful. Rather, Joseph is "doing good" to them that once hated and "despitefully used" him. He is saying, through his actions, "You are forgiven."

The next morning the sons of Jacob prepare to return home. Joseph again has a surprise for them. This time he has his steward place Joseph's silver cup into Benjamin's sack of corn and places in each of their sacks all of the money they had used to purchase food. Soon after they depart, Joseph sends the steward after them to accuse them once again of stealing from him. They are shocked at this and quickly open the sacks of grain to prove their innocence. They promise that if the cup is found in one of their bags, the owner of that bag of grain will die and the rest of them will become servants to the governor.

"And [Joseph's steward] said, Now also let it be according to your words: he with whom it is found shall be my servant; and ye shall be blameless. And they speedily took down every man his sack to the ground, and opened every man his sack. And he searched, and began at the eldest, and left at the youngest: and the cup was found in Benjamin's sack. And they rent their clothes . . . and returned to the city" (Genesis 44:10–13).

Upon arriving back in Joseph's court, Judah and his brothers fall to the ground before their brother. Judah recounts to Joseph all of the events that occurred up to the present, pleading with him to allow Benjamin to return home. In exchange, he offers himself as "surety" to take his younger brother's place as Joseph's servant. "For how shall I go up to my father, and the lad be not with me? Lest peradventure I see the evil that shall come on my father" (Genesis 44:34).

What was happening in the hearts of Judah and his brothers during this wrenching experience? Were the "pangs of guilt" that they had been carrying all of these years over their mistreatment of Joseph once again burning bright? Were they thinking that somehow this series of misfortunes was related to their sin against their brother twenty years earlier? Clearly they were still torn over their actions. And the scriptural record seems to indicate that they were still carrying the weight of their wickedness on their souls.

After listening to Judah plead Benjamin's cause, Joseph could no longer withstand the urge to reveal his identity to these men he had so clearly and completely forgiven:

Then Joseph could not refrain himself before all them that stood by him; and he cried, Cause every man to go out from me. And there stood no man with him, while Joseph made himself known unto his brethren.

And he wept aloud: and the Egyptians and the house of Pharaoh heard.

And Joseph said unto his brethren, I am Joseph; doth my father yet live? And his brethren could not answer him; for they were troubled at his presence.

And Joseph said unto his brethren, Come near to me, I pray you. And they came near. And he said, I am Joseph your brother, whom ye sold into Egypt.

Now therefore be not grieved, nor angry with yourselves, that ye sold me hither: for God did send me before you to preserve life.

For these two years hath the famine been in the land: and yet there are five years, in the which there shall neither be earing nor harvest.

And God sent me before you to preserve you a posterity in the earth, and to save your lives by a great deliverance.

So now it was not you that sent me hither, but God: and he hath made me a father to Pharaoh, and lord of all his house, and a ruler throughout all the land of Egypt.

Haste ye, and go up to my father, and say unto him, Thus saith thy son Joseph, God hath made me lord of all Egypt: come down unto me, tarry not:

And thou shalt dwell in the land of Goshen, and thou shalt be near unto me, thou, and

> thy children, and thy children's children, and thy flocks, and thy herds, and all that thou hast:
>
> And there will I nourish thee; for yet there are five years of famine; lest thou, and thy household, and all that thou hast, come to poverty.
>
> And, behold, your eyes see, and the eyes of my brother Benjamin, that it is my mouth that speaketh unto you.
>
> And ye shall tell my father of all my glory in Egypt, and of all that ye have seen; and ye shall haste and bring down my father hither.
>
> And he fell upon his brother Benjamin's neck, and wept; and Benjamin wept upon his neck.
>
> Moreover he kissed all his brethren, and wept upon them: and after that his brethren talked with him. (Genesis 45:1–15)

In the tender moment of revealing himself to his brothers, Joseph also reveals the beauty of his soul. What his brethren had done to him was unjust, unkind, and unfair. His response to what was done to him had always been to give "beauty for ashes," to treat others as they should have treated him, and to trust in God to make everything right. How healing this moment must have been for each of Jacob's sons. To see standing before them the brother that they surely thought they would never see again—whom they in anger and jealousy had treated so wrongfully—with tears of love streaming down his face no doubt filled their hearts with joy. Upon hearing of this sweet reunion, Pharaoh invites Jacob and all of his household to relocate to Goshen so that they might be closer to "the good of the land of Egypt."

"And they went up out of Egypt, and came into the land of Canaan unto Jacob their father, And told him, saying, Joseph is yet alive, and he is governor over all the land of Egypt. And Jacob's heart fainted, for he believed them not. And they told him all the words of Joseph, which he had said unto them: and when he saw the wagons which Joseph had sent to carry him, the spirit of Jacob their father revived: And Israel said, It is enough; Joseph my son is yet alive: I will go and see him before I die" (Genesis 45:25–28).

Joseph wasn't the only one who needed to forgive. His father also had to forgive his sons, both for what they'd done to Joseph and also because for twenty years they had deceived him about their role in Joseph's disappearance. Jacob too had to choose to respond in a Christlike way, just as Joseph had chosen to do. The moment of reunion then came. For both father and long-lost son, it was surely sweet. "And Joseph made ready his chariot, and went up to meet Israel his father, to Goshen, and presented himself unto him; and he fell on his neck, and wept on his neck a good while" (Genesis 46:29).

We learn only after Israel's death what his counsel was to Joseph concerning his mistreatment by his brothers. After Israel's body is buried in Canaan, Joseph's brothers are certain that now, at last, his day of vengeance has come. But Joseph has long since learned that holding a grudge is futile, unwise, and ultimately self-defeating.

> And when Joseph's brethren saw that their father was dead, they said, Joseph will peradventure hate us, and will certainly requite us all the evil which we did unto him.
>
> And they sent a messenger unto Joseph, saying, Thy father did command before he died, saying,
>
> So shall ye say unto Joseph, Forgive, I pray thee now, the trespass of thy brethren, and their sin; for they did unto thee evil: and now, we pray thee, forgive the trespass of the servants of

> the God of thy father. And Joseph wept when they spake unto him.
>
> And his brethren also went and fell down before his face; and they said, Behold, we be thy servants.
>
> And Joseph said unto them, Fear not: for am I in the place of God?
>
> But as for you, ye thought evil against me; but God meant it unto good, to bring to pass, as it is this day, to save much people alive.
>
> Now therefore fear ye not: I will nourish you, and your little ones. And he comforted them, and spake kindly unto them. (Genesis 50:15–21)

In reviewing this story through the lens of learning to give "beauty for ashes," we learn some important principles that are applicable to our present-day concerns and interactions. First, righteousness is not a guarantee of freedom from opposition. As the saying goes, "pain is inevitable, but misery is optional." Joseph wasn't spared adversity because he was innocent. In fact, it seems that his righteousness was the source, at least to some degree, of his brothers' anger toward him.

> Righteousness is not a guarantee of freedom from opposition.

Countless models, both prophetic and personal, confirm that this is a true principle. Nephi's brothers wanted to kill him because he didn't murmur against their father as they continually chose to do, and because they believed, falsely, that

Nephi wanted to rule over them. Joseph and Hyrum Smith, along with countless other early members of the Church, paid for their faith with their lives, their property, or both. Many other examples could be cited that teach us this truth. As Abraham learned in his vision of the council in heaven, the central purpose of mortality is for us to be tested: "And we will prove them herewith, to see if they will do all things whatsoever the Lord their God shall command them" (Abraham 3:25).

Second, we don't get to determine either the type or duration of our mortal tests. No doubt God could have intervened at any moment on Joseph's behalf to provide him with "justice" for the evil or unfair treatment he received. That was certainly within the powers of heaven. It also seems certain that Joseph "deserved" to be given justice for the "ashes" he was given. But as is also clear, the Lord's timing played a critical part in how and when Joseph was given "means unto . . . deliverance" (D&C 104:80). So it is with us. When we are in the middle of our misery, we too cry out, as did Joseph Smith from Liberty Jail,

> O God, where art thou? And where is the pavilion that covereth thy hiding place? How long shall thy hand be stayed, and thine eye, yea thy pure eye, behold from eternal heavens the wrongs of thy people and of thy servants, and thine ear be penetrated with their cries?
>
> Yea, O Lord, how long shall they suffer these wrongs and unlawful oppressions, before thine heart shall be softened toward them, and thy bowels be moved with compassion toward them? (D&C 121:1–3)

Indeed, hasn't the Lord repeatedly promised to "console [us] in [our] afflictions, and [that] he will plead [our] cause, and send down justice upon those who seek [our] destruction"?

(Jacob 2:1). Of course He has. And He will, and He does. But our rescue is always framed within the context and according to God's ultimate purpose, which is to "bring to pass the immortality and eternal life of man" (Moses 1:39). Thus His help often comes after our convictions and commitments have been tested, "for ye receive no witness until after the trial of your faith" (Ether 12:6).

Lastly, the trials and tests we experience are always intended to help us become more like the Savior. To live with Him, we must become more like Him. To know Him, we must experience the things He experienced. To love Him, we must learn to love the things that He loves. "For how knoweth the man the master whom he has not served, and who is a stranger unto him, and is far from the thoughts and intents of his heart?" (Mosiah 5:13). Loving as He loves includes especially loving those around us who may not be "lovable." It even includes those that have offended or attacked us. That is hard doctrine. But it is also the way mortality was designed to prove us.

> Trials and tests are always intended to help us become more like the Savior.

It took more than twenty years for Joseph to be shaped into the mighty man that he became. God was with him each and every step of the way. Heaven consecrated Joseph's adversity for his gain. Heaven is anxious to do the same for each of us. But we too must trust in the Lord's purposes for us and in the type and timing of the help He will ultimately and always extend. As another Joseph who was also cast unfairly into prison was reminded:

> Thy God shall stand by thee forever and ever. If thou art called to pass through tribulation; if thou art in perils among false brethren; if thou art in perils among robbers; if thou art in perils by land or by sea;
>
> If thou art accused with all manner of false accusations; if thine enemies fall upon thee; if they tear thee from the society of thy father and mother and brethren and sisters; and if with a drawn sword thine enemies tear thee from the bosom of thy wife, and of thine offspring, and thine elder son, although but six years of age, shall cling to thy garments, and shall say,
>
> My father, my father, why can't you stay with us? O, my father, what are the men going to do with you? and if then he shall be thrust from thee by the sword, and thou be dragged to prison, and thine enemies prowl around thee like wolves for the blood of the lamb;
>
> And if thou shouldst be cast into the pit, or into the hands of murderers, and the sentence of death passed upon thee; if thou be cast into the deep; if the billowing surge conspire against thee; if fierce winds become thine enemy; if the heavens gather blackness, and all the elements combine to hedge up the way; and above all, if the very jaws of hell shall gape open the mouth wide after thee, know thou, my son, that all these things shall give thee experience, and shall be for thy good.
>
> The Son of Man hath descended below them all. Art thou greater than he? (D&C 121:4–7)

Joseph of Egypt was able to consistently give "beauty for ashes" because his heart had undergone the "mighty change" spoken of by Alma. When those who mistreated him looked into his eyes, they saw, if only dimly, that he had been "spiritually born of God." They saw the image of Jesus Christ reflected in Joseph's countenance. Though they may not have recognized what or who they saw, in each and every instance, just as it can be for each of us, they sensed that there was something different, even holy, about this man. As President Ezra Taft Benson taught,

> The Lord works from the inside out. The world works from the outside in. The world would take people out of the slums. Christ takes the slums out of people, and then they take themselves out of the slums. The world would mold men by changing their environment. Christ changes men, who then change their environment. The world would shape human behavior, but Christ can change human nature.
>
> "Human nature *can* be changed, here and now," said President McKay, and then he quoted the following:
>
> "You can change human nature. No man who has felt in him the Spirit of Christ even for half a minute can deny this truth. . . .
>
> "You do change human nature, your own human nature, if you surrender it to Christ. Human nature has been changed in the past. Human nature must be changed on an enormous scale in the future, unless the world is to be drowned in its own blood. And only Christ can change it.
>
> "Twelve men did quite a lot to change the world nineteen hundred years ago. Twelve simple men." (Beverly Nichols, in David O. McKay,

Stepping Stones to an Abundant Life [Salt Lake City: Deseret Book, 1971], 23)

Yes, Christ changes men, and changed men can change the world. Men changed for Christ will be captained by Christ. Like Paul they will be asking, "Lord, what wilt thou have me to do?" (Acts 9:6). Peter stated they will "follow his steps." (1 Pet. 2:21). John said they will "walk, even as he walked." (1 Jn. 2:6).

Finally, men captained by Christ will be consumed in Christ. To paraphrase President Harold B. Lee, they set fire in others because they are on fire. (See Harold B. Lee, *Stand Ye in Holy Places* [Salt Lake City: Deseret Book, 1974], 192.) ("Born of God," Conference Report, Oct. 1985)

CHAPTER 5

"Of you it is required to forgive all men." —D&C 64:10

ONE OF THE IMMEDIATE CHALLENGES we face in our desire to become the Christlike response is the requirement to "forgive men their trespasses." This commandment is both universal and inescapable. There are neither exceptions nor exemptions. Forgiveness is a fundamental and essential part of the process of our becoming like the Savior. And of course, as in all things, He is the perfect model of how to forgive. Perhaps even more important, He is able to assist each of us through the sometimes long and arduous process of forgiving another person. His atoning power and enabling grace are sufficient to repair the breach that may exist between us and a brother or sister, no matter how wide the gap nor how grievous the offense.

This does not mean that forgiveness is easy. Quite the contrary. Not only must we say that we forgive another, but we must also experience the feeling of forgiveness toward him or her. This can be exceedingly difficult, especially when we are innocent of any wrong or if the person who has "trespassed" against us is unrepentant. But again, there are no exceptions.

As the Lord taught Joseph Smith,

> My disciples, in days of old, sought occasion against one another and forgave not one another in their hearts; and for this evil they were afflicted and sorely chastened.
>
> Wherefore, I say unto you, that ye ought to forgive one another; for he that forgiveth not his brother his trespasses standeth condemned before the Lord; for there remaineth in him the greater sin.
>
> I, the Lord, will forgive whom I will forgive, but of you it is required to forgive all men.
>
> And ye ought to say in your hearts—let God judge between me and thee, and reward thee according to thy deeds. (D&C 64:8–11)

Can what the Lord says here really be true? Can failing to forgive be a greater sin than whatever sin or offense was committed against us? How is such a thing possible? Perhaps part of the reason is because our choice not to forgive always stops our spiritual progress, regardless of how grievous the offense against us might have been. By holding on to a grudge or by continuing to harbor hurt feelings, we prevent the Savior's healing balm from quickening the process of soul repair that He is always ready and able to offer both the offended and the offender. Our unwillingness to forgive and to let go of wounded feelings stops or damns our progress. We become stuck in an ever-tightening circle of self-pity, self-deception, and anger. We're trapped in a ditch we've dug for ourselves. Only in reaching for the Savior's outstretched hand can we hope for rescue.

Brother C. Terry Warner shares the story of a friend who was in just such a predicament. Brother Warner's friend and a fellow ward member were at odds with each other, and the unspoken but ever-present tension this caused had endured over a long period, affecting not only the two men involved but also their families. Brother Warner's friend, whom he calls Brother Douglas, recounts the moment when he finally discovered his sin and at the same moment found freedom from the bondage of not forgiving another:

> I had intended to go over to this man's house between church meetings but was detained. Suddenly I saw this brother walk out of the church and cross the parking lot to his car. I cut short the conversation I was in and almost ran after him. When I caught up with him I put my hand on his shoulder from behind, turned him around, entwined our forearms, then pulled him close to me. When you pounce on someone like that it usually means that you have something important to say. But what was I supposed to say? I still wasn't sure what my offense was.
>
> It was not until the very moment I looked directly and deeply into this man's eyes for the first time in years that I could see my sin. At that moment I no longer saw him, I saw myself reflected! Where there had been no words to say, I found myself asking this good man for his forgiveness. "Why?" he asked. I heard myself reply, "Because I have loved you less. That is my sin: I have loved you less."
>
> Tears filled our eyes as I told him then that I loved him. He knew that I loved him. Whatever else I said after that really didn't matter much. I left him to return to the church. I

> glanced back once to see this good brother still standing where I had left him, his head down, and his shoulders gently rolling with his sobs. ("Honest. Simple. Solid. True," *BYU Speeches*, 1996)

This story teaches us in a powerful way the healing effect forgiveness can have both for offenders and for those offended against. Sadly, the opposite is also true. When we are unwilling to forgive, unwilling to "give beauty for ashes"—even when beauty isn't "deserved"—our progress is stopped and we are left to struggle in the ditch we dug with our own shovel, our hopes frail and dimming.

In his book *On Wings of Faith*, Brother Frederick W. Babbel recounts an experience that occurred during his service as an assistant to Elder Ezra Taft Benson in Europe immediately following World War II, Elder Benson represented the Church in offering assistance to the war-ravaged people across the European continent. In this particular account, Brother Babbel was in London providing priesthood blessings to members with a variety of ailments. As he relates it,

> The second person was a three-year-old boy from Scotland. He had been a deaf mute since birth. Now his parents had brought him to London for a special blessing. One of the brethren anointed his head with oil, and as I placed my hands upon his head to seal the anointing and to give him a blessing, I felt the Lord's power was present in such abundance that there was no question about his being healed instantly.
>
> After a moment's pause, I removed my hands from the boy's head and said to his parents, "What is it that you hate so deeply?"

> They looked startled. Then the husband said, "We can't tell you."
>
> "I don't need to know," I replied, "but as I placed my hands upon your son's head, I was assured that he might be healed this very night and be restored to you whole if you will only lose the hatred which you have in your hearts."
>
> After some troubled glances back and forth between the couple, the husband again spoke. "Well, if that is the case," he said, "our son will have to go through life as he is, because we won't give up our hating!"
>
> I felt that I had been prevented from pronouncing a blessing that might have resulted in the salvation of that entire family. (Frederick W. Babbel, *On Wings of Faith* [Salt Lake City: Bookcraft, 1972], 160–161)

How tragic! How wide was the rift between this couple and the healing that the Savior was offering them! Even more poignant, their son's infirmity seemed a terrible metaphor for their own unwillingness to hear the voice of the Lord inviting them to come unto Him that they might be made whole, just as they desired their little boy to be blessed and healed. "Will ye not now return unto me, and repent of your sins, and be converted, that I may heal you? Yea, verily, I say unto you, if ye will come unto me ye shall have eternal life. Behold, mine arm of mercy is extended towards you, and whosoever will come, him will I receive; and blessed are those who come unto me" (3 Nephi 9:13–14).

Finding the path to forgiveness is never a solo pursuit. We must constantly seek the assistance of the Savior as we walk toward our personal place of healing. Because He lived the principle of unconditional forgiveness, He is able to teach us and assist us in forgiving others. As Mormon taught, "And now, my brethren, how is it possible that ye can lay hold upon every good thing? And now I come to that faith, of which I said I would speak; and I will tell you the way whereby ye may lay hold on every good thing. For behold, God knowing all things . . . behold he sent angels to minister unto the children of men, to make manifest concerning the coming of Christ; and *in Christ there should come every good thing*" (Moroni 7:20–22; emphasis added).

When He tells us to love our enemies, He gives, along with the command, the love itself.

Perhaps one of the biggest traps we fall into as followers of Christ is our limited understanding of how comprehensive His grace can be. We often limit the Savior's ability to heal and to cleanse us because we inaccurately assume that His Atonement applies "only" to our being forgiven of our sins. It's as if we are standing at the base of a slight incline that's just high enough to obscure our being able to see Mt. Everest towering majestically behind the hill. Realizing that the Atonement of Jesus Christ covers everything is the first step to our understanding that He is both able and willing to guide us through the otherwise daunting experience of forgiving and being forgiven. The grace of Jesus Christ is sufficient.

A poignant example of this is captured in the life of Corrie ten Boom, author of *The Hiding Place*. Miss ten Boom and her family were victims of the Holocaust. She survived Ravensbruck, one of the many gruesome Nazi concentration camps. Her sister, Betsie, did not. After World War II, ten Boom traveled the world, speaking on the importance of forgiveness and reconciliation, even with those who were once considered her enemies. One evening in her travels she had a defining moment in which all that she represented and believed was put to the test.

> It was at a church service in Munich that I saw him, the former S.S. man who had stood guard at the shower room door in the processing center at Ravensbruck. He was the first of our actual jailers that I had seen since that time. And suddenly it was all there—the roomful of mocking men, the heaps of clothing, Betsie's pain-blanched face.
>
> He came up to me as the church was emptying, beaming and bowing. "How grateful I am for your message, Fraulein," he said. "To think that, as you say, He has washed my sins away!"
>
> His hand was thrust out to shake mine. And I, who had preached so often . . . the need to forgive, kept my hand at my side.
>
> Even as the angry, vengeful thoughts boiled through me, I saw the sin of them. Jesus Christ had died for this man; was I going to ask for more? *Lord Jesus, I prayed, forgive me and help me to forgive him.*
>
> I tried to smile, I struggled to raise my hand. I could not. I felt nothing, not the slightest spark of warmth or charity. And so again I breathed a silent prayer. Jesus, I cannot forgive him. Give me Your forgiveness.
>
> As I took his hand the most incredible thing happened. From my shoulder along my

> arm and through my hand a current seemed to pass from me to him, while into my heart sprang a love for this stranger that almost overwhelmed me.
>
> And so I discovered that it is not on our forgiveness any more than on our goodness that the world's healing hinges, but on His. *When He tells us to love our enemies, He gives, along with the command, the love itself.* (Corrie ten Boom, with John and Elizabeth Sherrill, *The Hiding Place* [New York: Bantam Books, 1971], 238; emphasis added)

"When He tells us to love our enemies, He gives, along with the command, the love itself." That is the power of Jesus Christ, manifested in His ability to help us give "beauty for ashes" in circumstances where we might otherwise not be able to do so. Obedience to the commandment to forgive does not preclude nor cancel out the importance of an offender receiving justice for his offense. Both mercy and justice must be satisfied. Our "heartwork" includes allowing the Savior to administer justice in His way and on His timetable.

In a talk given at BYU entitled "On Measuring Flour and Forgiveness," Brother Madison Sowell taught this important aspect of forgiveness:

> "To forgive another" does not imply "to disregard judgment." Certainly forgiving another does not mean that we hold in contempt the law of justice. In fact, Doctrine and Covenants 64:11 affirms that the one who forgives should embrace judgment and hold the transgressor—especially, I would argue, the serious offender—accountable for what he or she has done. Verse 11 states

> unequivocally: "And ye ought to say in your hearts—let God judge between me [the offended] and thee [the offender], and reward thee according to thy deeds." This latter phrase echoes the words of Paul regarding one who had done him "much evil." The apostle prays that "the Lord reward him according to his works" (2 Timothy 4:14), and this should be our prayer as well. But it must be a prayer uttered not in hatred, not in bitterness, but rather as "moved upon by the Holy Ghost" (D&C 121:43).
>
> To forgive a serious offense, in other words, is to turn in faith to God, to pray that he will help the offender repent, and to allow God to judge and reward. It means to accept humbly God's righteous judgment with faith, hope, and comfort, with joy and peace. I repeat: The concept of judgment is not jettisoned overboard by the commandment to forgive even serious offenders. Rather, to forgive is to turn over to God the ultimate right to judge and, *if* the offender refuses to repent, to allow Him to decree the final punishment. As Amulek witnessed to Zeezrom, not even God can save sinners "*in* their sins" (Alma 11:37; emphasis added). (Madison U. Sowell, "On Measuring Flour and Forgiveness," *BYU Speeches*, 1996)

Turning over this aspect of forgiveness to the Lord and allowing Him to replace our broken hearts with healing is an essential aspect of our becoming disciples of Christ. If we are to become "even as [He] is," then we must develop this ability to unconditionally forgive those who have hurt or offended us. Making our forgiveness conditional on whether or not the offender repents or first seeks our forgiveness is in fact not an act of forgiveness at all. As with most gospel principles, our understanding often precedes our application of what we know to be true. But this doesn't excuse us from making the effort, even when it requires rigorous and even painful soul stretching. As President Dieter F. Uchtdorf has taught,

> Developing Christlike attributes in our lives is not an easy task, especially when we move away from generalities and abstractions and begin to deal with real life. The test comes in practicing what we proclaim. The reality check comes when Christlike attributes need to become visible in our lives—as husband or wife, as father or mother, as son or daughter, in our friendships, in our employment, in our business, and in our recreation. We can recognize our growth, as can those around us, as we gradually increase our capacity to "act in all holiness before [Him]" (D&C 43:9). ("Developing Christlike Attributes," *Ensign*, Oct. 2008, 5–9)

The Savior can help us to forgive. He can teach us how to forgive. He stands ready to assist us in the often-difficult process of forgiving one another. If we will prayerfully ask a loving and wise Heavenly Father to send His Son to stand as our Mediator, He will surely hear and answer us.

> Listen to him who is the advocate with the Father, who is pleading your cause before him—
>
> Saying: Father, behold the sufferings and death of him who did no sin, in whom thou wast well pleased; behold the blood of thy Son

> which was shed, the blood of him whom thou gavest that thyself might be glorified;
>
> Wherefore, Father, spare these my brethren that believe on my name, that they may come unto me and have everlasting life. (D&C 45:2–4)

At the conclusion of his talk, Brother Sowell shared the following poem about being unconditionally forgiving. It is entitled "Forgiveness Flour." It beautifully captures the essence of true forgiveness:

> When I went to the door, at the whisper of knocking,
> I saw Simeon Gantner's daughter, Kathleen, standing
> There, in her shawl and her shame, sent to ask
> "Forgiveness Flour" for her bread. "Forgiveness Flour,"
> We call it in our corner. If one has erred, one
> Is sent to ask for flour of his neighbors. If they loan it
> To him, that means he can stay, but if they refuse, he had
> Best take himself off. I looked at Kathleen . . .
> What a jewel of a daughter, though not much like her
> Father, more's the pity. "I'll give you flour," I
> Said, and went to measure it. Measuring was the rub.
> If I gave too much, neighbors would think I made sin
> Easy, but if I gave too little, they would label me
> "Close." While I stood measuring, Joel, my husband

Came in from the mill, a great bag of flour on his
Shoulder, and seeing her there, shrinking in the
Doorway, he tossed the bag at her feet. "Here, take
All of it." And so she had flour for many loaves,
While I stood measuring.
(Marguerite Stewart, "Forgiveness Flour," *Religious Studies Center Newsletter* 7, no. 3 [May 1993]: 1)

CHAPTER 6

"These things have I spoken unto you, that ye should not be offended." —John 16:1

AN IMPORTANT PART OF FORGIVING others is choosing not to be offended. It's hard not to take offense when someone has said or done something we determine to be offensive. It's also true that we'll face many situations in life that could cause us to choose to take offense. The word *choose* is significant. No one can offend us unless we choose to let him or her offend us. This can be a hard truth to accept. We're far more comfortable with blaming others for our hurt feelings. Is there a cost to us for such thinking? Without question. By choosing to be offended by something someone has said or done to us, we limit our own ability to progress spiritually. If taking offense includes cutting ourselves off from the blessings of the gospel—such as not attending or serving in the Church or not partaking of other blessings offered to us—then this choice to take offense can quickly take on eternal significance.

In his talk, "And Nothing Shall Offend Them," given in the October 2006 general conference, Elder David A.

Bednar taught the following regarding our choosing to be offended:

> When we believe or say we have been offended, we usually mean we feel insulted, mistreated, snubbed, or disrespected. . . . However, it ultimately is impossible for another person to offend you or to offend me. Indeed, believing that another person offended us is fundamentally false. To be offended is a choice we make; it is not a condition inflicted or imposed upon us by someone or something else.
>
> To believe that someone or something can make us feel offended, angry, hurt, or bitter diminishes our moral agency and transforms us into objects to be acted upon. As agents, however, you and I have the power to act and to choose how we will respond to an offensive or hurtful situation.

As mentioned previously, the Savior can help us through the process of choosing not to be offended. This process is neither easy nor quick. But if we seek for the Lord's help, He can bless us with the ability to not take offense or to hold grudges. The word *grudge* is an interesting one. Some of its synonyms are *grievance*, *resentment*, *bitterness*, *rancor*, *pique*, *umbrage*, *dissatisfaction*, *disgruntlement*, *bad feelings*, *hard feelings*, *ill feelings*, *ill will*, *animosity*, *antipathy*, *antagonism*, *enmity*, and *animus*.

In the January 2006 issue of the *Ensign*, an anonymous author shared the following story about her struggle in choosing not to be offended.

> I couldn't believe my ears. A priesthood leader was standing at the pulpit in sacrament

> meeting, not mentioning me by name but publicly expressing his displeasure at the way I had handled a recent assignment with the youth. I remembered that when the calling came I hadn't felt skilled or confident, but believing that the Lord could make something of a willing heart, I accepted, prayed fervently, put in long hours, and did my best.
>
> Looking back, I realize that I fully expected Heavenly Father to put an arm around my injured pride and tell me, "Of course you are right!" I was, therefore, not prepared for the sweet, simple answer that came. It was a phrase from a poem I had heard long ago that landed softly on my agitated soul: "They are good, they are bad, . . . so am I." Although I couldn't remember the rest of the poem or even its title, the message was clear.
>
> I asked again, "Who is right?" This time I knew the answer: I am, and he is. "And who is wrong?" I am, and he is. . . . I realized that I needed to forgive because I had been forgiven many times, and it likely would not be long until I did something that would require forgiveness again. I decided to square my shoulders and support my priesthood leaders. These thoughts made my heart soar free from the burden of the grudge I had carried for weeks. ("He Offended Me!" *Ensign*, Jan. 2006, 18)

This story illustrates the importance of seeking the help of the Lord when someone has offended us. Even if things are not made "right" in the manner or at the time we might wish them to be, peace and freedom from resentment can still be ours. Notice that there is no mention made of this priesthood leader seeking out this sister to apologize for his offense. Was his approach to correction imperfect? It seems to be. Could he have instead followed the Savior's admonition, "Moreover, if thy brother [or sister] shall trespass against thee, go and tell him his fault *between him and thee alone*" (Matthew 18:15; emphasis added)? Such an approach would likely have been more productive and less hurtful to this good sister, who was seeking faithfully to do her best in a difficult and daunting assignment. All that being said, she still needed to forgive. She still had to choose not to be offended.

Elder Marion D. Hanks taught us how important this choice is in our quest to become unshakeable disciples of Jesus Christ:

> Christ's love was so pure that he gave his life for us: "Greater love hath no man than this, that a man lay down his life for his friends." (John 15:13). But there was another gift he bestowed while he was on the cross, a gift that further measured the magnitude of his great love: he forgave, and asked his Father to forgive, those who persecuted and crucified him.
>
> Was this act of forgiveness less difficult than sacrificing his mortal life? Was it less a test of his love? I do not know the answer. But I have felt that the ultimate form of love for God and men is forgiveness.
>
> Someone has written: ". . . the withholding of love is the negation of the spirit of Christ, the proof that we never knew him, that for us he lived in vain. It means that he suggested nothing in all our thoughts, that he inspired nothing in all our lives, that we were not once

near enough to him to be seized with the spell of his compassion for the world."

What is our response when we are offended, misunderstood, unfairly or unkindly treated, or sinned against, made an offender for a word, falsely accused, passed over, hurt by those we love, our offerings rejected? Do we resent, become bitter, hold a grudge? Or do we resolve the problem if we can, forgive, and rid ourselves of the burden?

The nature of our response to such situations may well determine the nature and quality of our lives, here and eternally. (Marion D. Hanks, "Forgiveness: The Ultimate Form of Love," *Ensign*, Jan. 1974, 28)

All of us have faced and will yet face situations in which we must choose not to take offense. Whether in our families, our neighborhoods, our communities, our wards, or countless other settings, at some point we'll be confronted with the challenge of whether to take offense. In these moments, we should never feel as if we must fight this war of the soul alone. The Savior stands ready to help us. He is the perfect example of choosing not to be offended, even when He

All of us have faced and will yet face situations in which we must choose not to take offense.

was without offense. Not only did He model how to give "beauty for ashes," He also offers us the ability and power to become more like Him, including learning to choose not to be offended.

Thoughtful reflection on the life of the Savior reveals that again and again He chose not to take offense, even in circumstances where He clearly would have been justified in doing so. From the earliest moments of His public ministry until the cruel, culminating hours on an ignominious cross, Jesus Christ never allowed the choices of those around Him to determine how He would respond. On what appears to be an almost daily basis, the Savior was confronted with the choice of whether to take offense. He consistently chose to avoid doing so. As we're taught in modern revelation, "He suffered temptations, *but gave no heed unto them*" (D&C 20:22; emphasis added). Lest we assume that the Savior was exempt from the daily tests that are common to our mortal experience, Paul reminds us, "Wherefore in all things it behoved him to be made like unto his brethren, that he might be a merciful and faithful high priest in things pertaining to God, to make reconciliation for the sins of the people. For in that he himself hath suffered being tempted, he is able to succor them that are tempted" (Hebrews 2:17–18).

Here are but a few of the many instances where the Lord could have been offended and yet chose not to be:

- After the Savior's forty days of fasting in the wilderness, Satan immediately came to tempt Him. Central to Satan's strategy was a devious assault on Christ's identity. At least twice he began his efforts to persuade the Lord to violate divine law by whispering, "If thou be the Son of God." These same words were later invoked by the Savior's crucifiers as He hung in agony on the cross: "And they that passed by reviled him, wagging their heads, and saying, Thou that destroyest the temple, and buildest it in three days, save thyself. If thou be the Son of God, come down from the cross" (Matthew 27:39–40).
- His authority to act in the name of the Father was repeatedly questioned.

- Instead of being praised for His good works and miraculous healings, He was instead accused of being "of the devil" or of seeking for glory. "And lo, he cometh unto his own, that salvation might come unto the children of men even through faith on his name; and even after all this they shall consider him a man, and say that he hath a devil, and shall scourge him, and shall crucify him" (Mosiah 3:9).
- His own community and friends turned against Him. Several of His disciples fled when He most needed their companionship. Even Peter at one point denied that he knew the Lord.
- He was repeatedly threatened with physical violence in spite of His never threatening anyone for believing or teaching differently than He did.
- Those placed in authority—such as the scribes, Pharisees, and Jewish rulers—relentlessly hounded and harassed the Savior until they ultimately brought Him to trial and were directly responsible for His crucifixion.

> From the beginning of His mortal mission, the Lord Jesus Christ chose never to take offense.

- Instead of rejoicing in His miracles and healing power, His enemies were jealous of His followers and disparaged His acts of kindness as "works of the devil."
- The hours leading up to his death were filled with opportunities for the Lord to take offense. The scriptures show that He was mocked, beaten, spit upon, abused, falsely accused, and even scourged. In exchange for freedom being given to a vile and sedi-

tious murderer, Barabbas, the Lord was betrayed by His own people as they blindly insisted that His innocent blood "be on us and on our children" (Matthew 27:25).

Without exception, the Savior stayed true to His mission, even when He was treated so cruelly by the very people He had come to save. From the beginning of His mortal mission, when He proclaimed that He had come to "give beauty for ashes," until His final heartbreaking utterance—"It is finished"—the Lord Jesus Christ chose never to take offense. He invites us to "Go, and do thou likewise." Better still, He stands ready to heal our bruised and broken hearts, even when those who have offended us are unwilling to repair the breach their actions have caused. He is also able to mediate between offended parties, softening hearts, modeling how to forgive, and extending "help in time of need" (Hebrews 4:16).

> We can retain our freedom by choosing not to be a victim.

In Viktor Frankl's classic book, *Man's Search for Meaning*, the author chronicles his experiences in a Nazi concentration camp during World War II and details his discovery of the principle that allowed some of the victims of that atrocity not only to survive but also to thrive. Without providing a detailed summary of the book, perhaps two statements made by the author will suffice to make the intended point.

During Frankl's time in the concentration camp, he attempted to discover a way of making meaning out of the inhumane treatment and subsequent genocide being committed against his own people. His training led him to the following insights as he observed fellow prisoners either perish or survive.

He concluded that "everything can be taken from a man or a woman but one thing: the last of human freedoms to choose one's attitude in any given set of circumstances, to choose one's own way" (Boston, Massachusetts: Beacon Press, 1984, 66.)

This would seem to be our experience in circumstances in which we're offended or hurt by someone. We too are able to choose our attitude regardless of the circumstances in which we find ourselves. We too have the freedom to decide how we will respond, no matter how hurtful another has been to us. As President Thomas S. Monson wrote, "So much in life depends on our attitude. The way we choose to see things and respond to others makes all the difference. To do the best we can and then to choose to be happy about our circumstances, whatever they may be, can bring peace and contentment" ("Living the Abundant Life," *Ensign*, Jan. 2012, 2).

A second but equally important insight shared by Frankl is the following: "Between stimulus and response there is a space. In that space is our power to choose our response. In our response lies our growth and our freedom" (Ibid., 68). This idea of a space or gap is a profoundly important one. Understanding that we always have the ability to choose our response can fundamentally alter our relationships. Rather than feeling that we are the victims in circumstances where we've been mistreated, we can instead retain our freedom by choosing not to be a victim.

We cannot fully control nor prevent the things that happen to us in life. A significant part of our mortal experience is just that: experience. We must "get through" difficult and even heartbreaking mortal struggles in order to develop the Christlike nature we were sent to earth to acquire.

Being in circumstances where we could easily be offended is a central facet of our mortal experience. The Savior Himself prophesied that the trials of life and our response to them would be a necessary part of the last days. "And then shall many be offended, and shall betray one another, and shall hate one another" (Joseph Smith—Matthew 1:8). Gratefully, we have the proffered help of heaven to assist us in successfully negotiating the almost constant mortal storms that sometimes beset us. The devil would have us choose to be offended, which ultimately hurts us far more than it does the offender.

Elder Bednar once shared that as a priesthood leader, he'd visited with hundreds of people who had chosen to take offense because of something a Church member had done to offend them:

One of my favorite activities as a priesthood leader is visiting members of the Church in their homes. I especially enjoy calling upon and talking with members who commonly are described as "less active." . . .

> I made hundreds and hundreds of such visits. Each individual, each family, each home, and each answer was different. Over the years, however, I detected a common theme in many of the answers to my questions. Frequently responses like these were given:
>
> "Several years ago a man said something in Sunday School that offended me, and I have not been back since."
>
> "No one in this branch greeted or reached out to me. I felt like an outsider. I was hurt by the unfriendliness of this branch."
>
> "I did not agree with the counsel the bishop gave me. I will not step foot in that building again as long as he is serving in that position."

Many other causes of offense were cited—from doctrinal differences among adults to taunting, teasing, and excluding by youth. But the recurring theme was: "I was offended by . . ."

After listening to those that had been offended, Elder Bednar would then ask them the following question:

> Let me make sure I understand what has happened to you. Because someone at church offended you, you have not been blessed by the ordinance of the sacrament. You have withdrawn yourself from the constant companionship of the Holy Ghost. Because someone at church offended you, you have cut yourself off from priesthood ordinances and the holy temple. You have discontinued your opportunity to serve others and to learn and grow. And you are leaving barriers that will impede the spiritual progress of your children, your children's children, and the generations that will follow." Many times people would think for a moment and then respond: "I have never thought about it that way." (David A. Bednar, "And Nothing Shall Offend Them," *Ensign*, Oct. 2006, 38).

Clearly a critical part of learning to give "beauty for ashes" is learning not to take offense. As followers of Jesus Christ, we are provided the ability to resist this common human impulse through our Savior's enabling grace, as we are with all other Christlike characteristics. In circumstances where we face the difficult choice of whether to take offense, we must plead for heavenly assistance:

> Likewise the Spirit also helpeth our infirmities: for we know not what we should pray for as we ought: but the Spirit itself maketh intercession for us with groanings which cannot be uttered. And he that searcheth the hearts knoweth what is the mind of the Spirit, because he maketh intercession for the saints according to the will of God. And we know that all things work to-

> gether for good to them that love God, to them who are the called according to his purpose. (Romans 8:26–28)

Approaching heaven with a prayerful, pleading heart and with a willingness to submit ourselves to the will of God will provide meaningful, powerful protection against this common human frailty. As we carefully read the story of Nephi, we learn that one of the most important differences between him and his older brothers was Nephi's humility in prayer. After observing how offended Laman and Lemuel were by their father's claims of revelation, Nephi relates that he "did cry unto the Lord; and behold he did visit me, and did soften my heart that I did believe all the words which had been spoken by my father; wherefore, I did not rebel against him like unto my brothers" (1 Nephi 2:16). Later, when Nephi confronts his brothers over their incessant murmuring, he marvels at their stubborn unwillingness to "inquire of the Lord": "Yea, and how is it that ye have forgotten that the Lord is able to do all things for his will, for the children of men, if it so be that they exercise faith in him? Wherefore, let us be faithful to him" (1 Nephi 7:12).

CHAPTER 7

"The effectual fervent prayer of a righteous man availeth much."
—James 5:16

ELDER F. ENZIO BUSCHE SHARED the following experience he had as a parent that taught him the power of prayer when responding to challenges in a Christlike way:

> One day when circumstances made it necessary for me to be at home at an unusual time, I witnessed from another room how our eleven-year-old son, just returning from school, was directing ugly words towards his younger sister. They were words that offended me—words that I had never thought our son would use. My first natural reaction in my anger was to get up and go after him. Fortunately, I had to walk across the room and open a door before I could reach him, and I remember in those few seconds I fervently prayed to my Heavenly Father to help me to handle the situation. Peace came over me. I was no longer angry.

> Our son, being shocked to see me home, was filled with fear when I approached him. To my surprise I heard myself saying, "Welcome home, son!" and I extended my hand as a greeting. And then in a formal style I invited him to sit close to me in the living room for a personal talk. I heard myself expressing my love for him. I talked with him about the battle that every one of us has to fight each day within ourselves.
>
> As I expressed my confidence in him, he broke into tears, confessing his unworthiness and condemning himself beyond measure. Now it was my role to put his transgression in the proper perspective and to comfort him. A wonderful spirit came over us, and we ended up crying together, hugging each other in love and finally in joy. *What could have been a disastrous confrontation between father and son became, through the help from the powers above, one of the most beautiful experiences of our relationship that we both have never forgotten.* ("Love Is the Power That Will Cure the Family," *Ensign*, Apr. 1982; emphasis added)

As has been repeatedly emphasized throughout the pages of this book, the grand key that leads us to become "beauty for ashes" is a strong, abiding relationship with our Heavenly Father and with His Son, Jesus Christ. This relationship is what undergirds and surrounds all other human relationships. Truly, if we are lovingly grounded in covenantal obedience to the Savior, we will be incapable of being anything other than "even as He is." The Savior's tender and intimate relationship with His Father reaffirms this truth. As He taught His disciples, "Verily, verily, I say unto you, The Son can do nothing of himself, but what he seeth the Father do: for what things soever he doeth, these also doeth the Son likewise" (John 5:19). The depths and nuances of this verse are far beyond the scope of this book. Suffice it to say that I believe that the Lord is teaching us that the source of His power was the intimate proximity He had to His Father and His absolute "at one ment" with Him.

> I am the true vine, and my Father is the husbandman.
>
> Every branch in me that beareth not fruit he taketh away: and every branch that beareth fruit, he purgeth it, that it may bring forth more fruit.
>
> Now ye are clean through the word which I have spoken unto you.
>
> Abide in me, and I in you. As the branch cannot bear fruit of itself, except it abide in the vine; no more can ye, except ye abide in me.
>
> I am the vine, ye are the branches: He that abideth in me, and I in him, the same bringeth forth much fruit: for without me ye can do nothing. (John 15:1–5)

Here the Lord is teaching all prospective disciples that the only way we can "bear fruit" is through abiding in Him. I know of no more powerful way to remain firmly bound to the Savior than through "effectual fervent prayer." Coupled with frequent study of the scriptures and the words of living prophets, this practice of seeking to stay prayerfully linked to the "true vine" is central to our desire to become Christlike in all our responses to "ashes," regardless of their source or severity.

Perhaps because we so frequently hear and read admonitions to pray and to study the gospel, we may at times take such exhortations lightly. Such a practice is not without consequence.

The scriptures are rich with references to the importance of frequent prayer and diligent study. No doubt we are familiar with many of these, having heard or read them on more than one occasion. For those that have developed and are maintaining the practice of prayer and scripture study, elaborating on the benefits of such habits is unnecessary. As the Savior taught in the passage just cited, "He that abideth in me, and I in him, the same bringeth forth *much fruit*, for without me ye can do nothing" (John 15:5; emphasis added). Later in this same discourse He teaches that "If ye abide in me, and my words abide in you, ye shall ask what ye will, and it shall be done unto you" (v. 7).

The Bible Dictionary includes a beautiful insight on the efficacy and power of prayer as heaven's designated way for obtaining divine assistance:

> Prayer is the act by which the will of the Father and the will of the child are brought into correspondence with each other. The object of prayer is not to change the will of God, but to secure for ourselves and for others blessings that God is already willing to grant, but that are made conditional on our asking for them.
>
> Blessings require some work or effort on our part before we can obtain them. Prayer is a form of work, and is an appointed means for obtaining the highest of all blessings. ("Prayer," 752–753)

Included on our list of "the highest of all blessings" would be the blessing of unity, even "at-one-ment" with our family members, friends, and others with whom we associate. How can we expect God to help us obtain such a blessing if we are not willing to ask Him for it? Likewise, we can't expect Him to grant us such a gift if we "take no thought save it [were] to ask [Him]" (D&C 9:7). Diligent prayer coupled with striving to "liken all scriptures unto [ourselves] that it might be for our profit and learning" (1 Nephi 19:23) is the divinely appointed means through which we obtain "every needful thing."

Truman G. Madsen recounted a tender incident from Church history when the efficacy and heart-changing power of prayer was affirmed. He related that during a meeting of the School of the Prophets in Kirtland, Ohio, Heber C. Kimball told of an experience that had recently occurred in his family:

> My daughter, Helen Mar, was standing near the table, and her mother left her saying, "Don't touch those dishes. Don't break one of those or I will whip you. Vilate left, and Helen Mar did what little children often do when they are told not to do it. Not just a dish was broken. The whole table leaf collapsed. All were broken.
>
> Now she went out, as she had watched her parents do, near a tree. We don't know what she said, but it would have been simple enough: "Bless my mother that she won't whip me."
>
> Vilate returned. She saw the situation. She flared. She led the little girl by the hand into the bedroom. She assumed the angle. And then she couldn't go through with it. And the arms of Helen Mar came around her neck, and she said, "Oh, mother, I prayed that you wouldn't. I'm sorry, sorry."
>
> When Brother Heber finished, every man in the room, including Joseph, was in tears. And Joseph said, "Brethren [these are grown-up, strong, independent, willful, intelligent men], that is the kind of faith we need, the

> faith of a little child going in humility to its Parent." (Orson F. Whitney, *Life of Heber C. Kimball* [Salt Lake City: Bookcraft, 1992], 69–79, as quoted in Truman G. Madsen, *The Radiant Life* [Salt Lake City: Bookcraft, 1994], 9)

We live far beneath our privileges when it comes to prayer. Again, perhaps because it is something we are reminded so frequently to do, there is real danger in our taking this supernal blessing for granted. We are invited, even commanded, to "pray always." To realize that God is pleading with us to prayerfully plead for help, for blessings, for whatsoever things we stand in need of, should fill our souls with rejoicing. Especially in our struggles to forgive, to not take offense, or to respond to conflict or confrontations in a Christlike way, prayer can truly "change the night to day."

> Ere you left your room this morning,
> Did you think to pray?
> In the name of Christ our Savior,
> Did you sue for loving favor,
> As a shield today?
>
> When your heart was filled with anger,
> Did you think to pray?
> Did you plead for grace, my brother,
> That you might forgive another
> Who had crossed your way?
>
> When sore trials came upon you,
> Did you think to pray?
> When your soul was full of sorrow,
> Balm of Gilead did you borrow
> At the gates of day?
> O how praying rests the weary!

Prayer will change the night to day;
So when life seems dark and dreary,
Don't forget to pray.
("Did You Think to Pray?" *Hymns*, no. 140)

One of the ways we discover the value of prayer as it relates to our becoming more Christlike is by experiencing life without prayer. All of us have likely experienced periods when our prayer life was lacking. I know I certainly have. At one point in my life I was struggling with several personal and family challenges, including problems with children and lack of employment. I'm confident I was still praying every day, but my prayers were warmed-over and routine. Somehow I had forgotten the vitality and power that is offered to those that strive for "long strugglings" in their petitions.

One day I was reminded of the Lord's admonition regarding praying "in Spirit," as given to Joseph Smith: "And it shall come to pass that he that asketh in Spirit shall receive in Spirit . . . He that asketh in the Spirit asketh according to the will of God; wherefore it is done even as he asketh" (D&C 46:28, 30). Instead of kneeling and asking again and again for what I wanted or "needed," I instead began to pray for the Spirit to teach me to pray. As Paul taught, "Likewise the Spirit also helpeth our infirmities: for we know not what we should pray for as we ought: but the Spirit itself maketh intercession for us with groanings which cannot be uttered" (Romans 8:26). The idea of the Spirit making intercession for us as we pray is a profound and important one. We need not, indeed must not, approach our Heavenly Father with a heart that is unprepared for the privilege of speaking with Him.

If we would know Him as He really is, prayer is our Heavenly Father's intended way for us to enter His presence. President Ezra Taft Benson once made this statement about how our Father is far closer to us than we realize and how familiar His face will be at our moment of postmortal reunion:

> We once knew well our Elder Brother and His and our Father in Heaven.
>
> We rejoiced at the prospects of earth life that could make it possible for us to have a fulness of joy. We could hardly wait to demonstrate to our Father and our Brother, the Lord, how much we loved them and how we would be obedient to them in spite of the earthly opposition of the evil one.
>
> Now we are here. Our memories are veiled. We are showing God and ourselves what we can do. Nothing is going to startle us more when we pass through the veil to the other side than to realize how well we know our Father and how familiar His face is to us ("Jesus Christ: Gifts & Expectations," *Ensign*, Dec. 1988, 4)

In our struggles to deal with hardships and day-to-day battles, prayer is God's way of providing us with the power to endure and ultimately triumph over mortal opposition. No wonder the adversary works so hard to get us to forget to pray:

> For if ye would hearken unto the Spirit which teacheth a man to pray, ye would know that ye must pray; for the evil spirit teacheth not a man to pray, but teacheth him that he must not pray.
>
> But behold, I say unto you that ye must pray always, and not faint; that ye must not perform any thing unto the Lord save in the first place ye shall pray unto the Father in the name of Christ, that he will consecrate thy performance unto thee, that thy performance may be for the welfare of thy soul. (2 Nephi 32:8–9)

> In our day-to-day battles, prayer is God's way of providing us with the power to endure and ultimately triumph.

During my service as a bishop, I saw again and again the real and hurtful consequences of losing one's prayerful connection to a loving Heavenly Father. Faithful and otherwise striving Latter-day Saints would come seeking counsel from their bishop as they struggled in their marriages, as parents, or in their Church callings. At some point in our conversation I would ask how they were doing spiritually. Most would indicate that they were "working" on doing better. No doubt all of us could improve in this aspect of our lives. But those who were in serious spiritual danger were always those who felt that prayer had little, if any, benefit for them. They'd been in a crisis of some kind or another at some point and had felt that heaven had been sealed to them. When they most needed God, they felt He wasn't "available." Or, as was more often the case, they felt unworthy of approaching Him to plead for blessings they so desperately wanted and yet felt no confidence in asking for. I would try to remind them that prayer was always the first step of repentance, and that just as they wouldn't turn an errant but humble child away if she came seeking assistance, so a perfect and all-loving Father would lovingly draw them back into His "arms of mercy." The look of doubt in their eyes was always heart-wrenching.

Eventually, if they chose not to change course, they ended up in my office or in a stake disciplinary council with their

Church membership at stake. As I or another leader would visit with them about what had brought them to that moment, without exception they would indicate that they had stopped praying, had stopped studying their scriptures, had in fact set aside all of the protections available to them. The following sobering verse of scripture from the Book of Mormon had been confirmed in their current circumstances:

> And now, my sons, remember, remember that it is upon the rock of our Redeemer, who is Christ, the Son of God, that ye must build your foundation; that when the devil shall send forth his mighty winds, yea, his shafts in the whirlwind, yea, when all his hail and his mighty storm shall beat upon you, it shall have no power over you to drag you down to the gulf of misery and endless wo, because of the rock upon which ye are built, which is a sure foundation, a foundation whereon if men build they cannot fall. (Helaman 5:12)

They had indeed felt the devil's "mighty winds, yea his shafts in the whirlwind." They had personally experienced "his mighty storm" as they ceased to call upon God for deliverance, instead relying on "the arm of flesh" to help them through the torrent. Prayer is the rudder used by the Lord to help us successfully navigate our various relationship challenges. If we set aside the blessing of prayer, thinking it no longer has relevance to our daily walk, we do so at the peril of our souls.

Elder Boyd K. Packer emphasized the importance of nurturing our personal relationship with God in a talk he gave at BYU. He later gave a shorter version of the same address in the April 1978 general conference and titled his remarks "Solving Emotional Problems the Lord's Own Way." In both addresses he spoke of how many bishops in the Church kept so-called "emotional welfare" forms on their desk to hand out to members coming to them in distress. He warned of the dangers of this practice, as it often led members to become spiritually dependent on their bishop's counsel rather than them learning to become spiritually and emotionally "self-reliant."

> I have been concerned that we may be on the verge of doing to ourselves emotionally (and therefore spiritually) what we have been working so hard for generations to avoid materially. If we lose our emotional and spiritual self-reliance, we can be weakened quite as much, perhaps even more, than when we become dependent materially. On the one hand, we counsel bishops to avoid abuses in the Church welfare program. On the other hand, we seem to dole out counsel and advice without the slightest thought that the member should solve the problem himself or turn to his family. . . . If we are not careful, we can lose power of individual revelation.

He went on to suggest a cure for such spiritual dependence:

> When you have a problem, work it out in your own mind first. Ponder on it and analyze it and meditate on it. Pray about it. I've come to learn that major decisions can't be forced. You must look ahead and have vision. What was it the prophet said in the Old Testament? "Where there is no vision, the people perish" (Proverbs 29:18). . . .
>
> I have learned that the best time to wrestle with major problems is early in the morning.

> Your mind is fresh and alert. The blackboard of your mind has been erased by a good night's rest. The accumulated distractions of the day are not in your way. Your body has been rested also. That's the time to think something through very carefully and to receive personal revelation. . . .
>
> The Lord knew something when He directed in the Doctrine and Covenants, "Cease to sleep longer than is needful; retire to thy bed early, that ye may not be weary; arise early, that your bodies and your minds may be invigorated" (D&C 88:124). . . .
>
> I counsel our children to do their critical studying in the early hours of the morning when they're fresh and alert, rather than to fight the physical weariness and mental exhaustion at night. I've learned that the dictum "Early to bed, early to rise" is powerful. When under pressure—for instance, when I was preparing this talk—you wouldn't find me burning the midnight oil. Much rather I'd be early to bed and getting up in the wee hours of the morning, when I could be close to Him who guides this work . . . you have great and powerful resources. You, through prayer, can solve your problems without endlessly going to those who are trying so hard to help others. ("Self Reliance," *BYU Speeches*, March 2, 1975)

How does prayer help us in our efforts to become more Christlike? How does it affect our ability to give "beauty for ashes"? A good example can be found in the story of Enos in the Book of Mormon. As the account begins, Enos, the son of Jacob, is on a hunting excursion into the forest. His mind is preoccupied with the "words which I had often heard my father speak concerning eternal life, and the joy of the saints" (Enos 1:3). As he ponders the principles he has been taught, his soul hungers to make his own connection with God. As he relates, "I kneeled down before my Maker, and I cried unto him in mighty prayer and supplication for mine own soul; and all the day long did I cry unto him; yea, and when the night came I did still raise my voice high that it reached the heavens" (Enos 1:4).

After such unwavering faith, the heavens at last are opened and Enos hears a voice saying that his sins are forgiven him. Instantly his guilt is swept away. He instinctively wants to understand how this is done and asks for more understanding. In reply, he is told that this great blessing has come "because of thy faith in Christ, whom thou hast never before heard nor seen . . . wherefore, go to, thy faith hath made thee whole." (Enos 1:8).

What Enos felt next is directly related to our own experience of trying to become more like the Savior. He shared that when he heard his sins had been forgiven and that his faith in Christ had made him whole, he began "to feel a desire for the welfare of [his] brethren, the Nephites; wherefore, I did pour out my whole soul unto God for them." Nothing remarkable here, is there? Enos is a Nephite, after all. It makes perfect sense that he would feel a desire to pray for his own people, wouldn't it?

The account continues. Enos shares the words spoken to him by the Lord, indicating that if the Nephites will be obedient they will be blessed, and if disobedient, cursed. "And after I, Enos, had heard these words, my faith began to be unshaken in the Lord; and I prayed unto him with many long strugglings for my brethren, *the Lamanites*. And it came to pass after I had prayed and labored with all diligence, the Lord said unto me: I will grant unto thee according to thy desires, because of thy faith" (Enos 1:11; emphasis added).

It is a comparatively easy thing for us to pray for ourselves, our families, and those we love and care for. It is quite another thing for us to pray sincerely, even pleading in "long strugglings," for our enemies. But that is exactly what Enos models for us here. The Lamanites and the Nephites hated each other. They were constantly at war, seeking to shed one another's blood. And yet here is Enos, pleading in prayer for the Lamanites to somehow be reclaimed and restored to a state of brotherhood with the Nephites. The sequence is significant. Enos first needed to have his own heart changed before he was able to sincerely seek blessings for his "enemies." Once he had received that "mighty change of heart," his first desire was for the welfare of those with whom his people had been so long estranged.

Prayer: the Lord's appointed way for a mighty change of heart to occur.

We likewise can experience this powerful change in our own hearts. Prayer is the Lord's appointed means for this to occur. There is a soothing, healing balm in the quiet pleadings of the heart. As we approach the throne of grace, humble and submissive, our loving Father stands ready to take the anger from our hearts. As discussed earlier, the Anti-Nephi-Lehies experienced this change in their spiritual countenances. Their king reminds them that only through prayerful repentance were they able "to get God to take [the many murders] away from [their] hearts, for it was all [they] could do to repent sufficiently before God that he would take away [their] stain" (Alma 24:11). There is a wonderful story told about Brigham Young modeling the power of prayer to help him overcome a flash of anger. It was related by his daughter, Emma Lucy Gates, to Hugh Nibley:

> There is one story I must tell because it is strictly firsthand; I heard it from Emma Lucy during a

> dinner at her home when I first came to Utah. There used to be a barn behind the Lion House where Brother Brigham kept his horses. One day when Emma Lucy was nine years old she heard her father out in the barn giving the grooms a royal dressing down for having allowed a fine saddle to fall from its peg to the floor where it got trampled in the dirt. She waited until Brigham came back to the house and stormed down the hall to his office. Then she listened at the door and actually heard him say, "Down on your knees Brigham! Get down on your knees!" He was ashamed of himself for having embarrassed the grooms and so lost control over his temper. He recommended that the Brethren keep handy a piece of India rubber to chew whenever they got angry to avoid swearing. ("Exemplary Manhood," chapter 19 in Collected Works of Hugh Nibley, vol. 13: *Brother Brigham Challenges the Saints* [Provo, Utah: BYU Publications, 1994])

In Brigham's own words, "I will say, there is not a man in this house who has a more indomitable and unyielding temper than myself. But there is not a man in the world who cannot overcome his passion, if he will struggle earnestly to do so. If you find passion coming on you, go off to someplace where you cannot be heard; let none of your family see you or hear you, while it is upon you, but struggle till it leaves you; and pray for strength to overcome" (*Journal of Discourses*, 11:290).

Countless additional passages of scripture could be cited affirming the importance of prayer as it relates to our overcoming angry feelings, offending actions, or broken hearts. Prayer is indeed the "balm of Gilead" as was lamented by Jeremiah (see Jeremiah 8:22). As Elder Boyd K. Packer taught,

> The Bible records that in ancient times there came from Gilead, beyond the Jordan, a substance used to heal and soothe. It came, perhaps, from a tree or shrub, and was a major commodity of trade in the ancient world. It was known as the Balm of Gilead. That name became symbolic for the power to soothe and heal.
>
> The lyrics of a song record:
>
> There is a Balm in Gilead,
> To make the wounded whole,
> There is a Balm in Gilead,
> To heal the sin sick soul.
>
> ("There Is a Balm in Gilead," *Recreational Songs* [Salt Lake City: The Church of Jesus Christ of Latter-day Saints, 1949], 130)

In his October 1977 general conference talk titled "The Balm of Gilead," Elder Packer recounted the experience of a close friend and mentor who had learned firsthand the power of prayer and forgiveness from a "beauty for ashes" experience that could have easily destroyed his life. He told the story of a saintly man whose spiritual strength inspired many. He had married a beautiful woman, had a good job, and a bright future. He and his wife were expecting their first child.

There were complications the night the baby was to be born, and they were unable to find the only doctor in the area, who was out in the countryside tending to someone who was ill. When the doctor finally arrived, the condition of the mother-to-be had become desperate. The doctor, accurately assessing the situation, acted quickly and decisively, and the baby was saved. It looked as if all was well.

Then the mother died from the same infection the doctor had been treating at the other home that night.

The man's world was shattered. He had lost his sweetheart, and he had no way to continue working and to take care of a newborn baby. Elder Packer said,

> As the weeks wore on his grief festered. "That doctor should not be allowed to practice," he would say. "He brought that infection to my wife; if he had been careful she would be alive today." He thought of little else, and in his bitterness he became threatening.
>
> Then one night a knock came at his door. A little youngster said, simply, "Daddy wants you to come over. He wants to talk to you."
>
> "Daddy" was the stake president. A grieving, heartbroken young man went to see his spiritual leader. This spiritual shepherd had been watching his flock and had something to say to him.

The stake president's counsel was simple: "John, leave it alone. Nothing you do about it will bring her back. Anything you do will make it worse. John, leave it alone."

He didn't understand how he could leave it alone. Right was right! He felt that a terrible wrong had been committed, and he also felt that somebody needed to pay for it.

He struggled in agony to overcome his feelings, but finally decided to follow the counsel of that wise stake president. He decided he would leave it alone. It took a number of years, but he succeeded. In his words, he was an old man before he finally understood that the doctor had done his best. And many a time he thanked the Lord for the wise counsel to simply "leave it alone."

Elder Packer continued:

> Often, however, the things we carry are petty, even stupid. If you are still upset after all these years because Aunt Clara didn't come to your wedding reception, why don't you grow up? Forget it.
>
> If you brood constantly over some past mistake, settle it—look ahead.
>
> If the bishop didn't call you right—or release you right—forget it.
>
> If you resent someone for something he has done—or failed to do—forget it.
>
> We call that forgiveness. It is powerful, spiritual medicine. The instructions for its use are found in the scriptures.
>
> I repeat: John, leave it alone. Mary, leave it alone. Purge and cleanse and soothe your soul and your heart and your mind.
>
> It will then be as though a cloudy, dirty film has been erased from the world around you; and though the problem may remain, the sun will come out. The beam will have been lifted from your eyes. There will come a peace that surpasseth understanding. (Boyd K. Packer, "The Balm of Gilead," *Ensign*, Nov. 1977)

If we will stretch beyond our blinding self-centeredness, we will feel our Heavenly Father's call to prayer. How He is able to both hear and answer prayers is beyond our current comprehension. Understanding how prayer works is secondary to simply knowing that it does work. If we will approach our Father and pray for Him to teach us how to pray, we will be well on our way to true and enduring healing. Over the course of our lives, the time spent on our knees in quiet, "long strugglings" will in summary be the very time in which we ultimately come to know and recognize the voice of True Love. "And rend your heart . . . and turn unto the Lord your God: for he is gracious and merciful, slow to anger, and of great kindness" (Joel 2:13).

CHAPTER 8

"The word which healeth the wounded soul." —Jacob 2:8

TIGHTLY INTERWOVEN WITH PRAYER IS the practice of a searching, diligent study of the scriptures. In relation to the development of Christlike character attributes, these two habits of the heart yield much peaceable fruit. In the ongoing and never-ending process of becoming "beauty for ashes," meaningful, focused time spent in the scriptures will draw us gradually and inevitably toward our desire to do and to be "even as [He] is" in all of our dealings and associations. If prayer is our personal Liahona, providing us with consistent direction as we journey toward our individual promised land, then regular scripture study is the act of "continually holding fast" to the iron rod as it leads us toward the tree of life.

Personal scripture study is a gospel habit that is easy to neglect. Because it is "personal," we sometimes lack the motivation or discipline to keep at it, instead easily finding other more interesting or entertaining activities to occupy our unscheduled time. It is also easy to defer the quiet reminders that come from the Spirit, encouraging us to spend personal time in scripture study, as we instead promise that we'll be sure to do that "later," when things aren't quite so hectic and stressful. Somehow the "free time" we were sure would eventually happen never quite arrives. Sadly, we're also less likely to make the commitment necessary to persist in striving to make time for scripture study when there is stress or conflict in our lives, which can be almost constant. With sincere intent we promise ourselves that we'll "get around to it" when things have quieted down, once we've resolved whatever problems or difficulties are currently facing us.

Ironically, the practice of meaningful study of the scriptures can often be the very catalyst needed to powerfully resolve the difficulties we may be facing in a relationship or other personal challenge. When we make the connection between the personal time we spend in the scriptures and the power and perspective that come to us in every other part of our lives as the result of scripture study, then the difficulty we experience in making the commitment and following through will likely diminish or disappear altogether.

In the Book of Mormon there are several accounts of how powerful the scriptures can be in helping us overcome our many personal and relationship challenges. In Alma we read the story of Alma the Younger and several of his brethren as they set out on a mission to the Lamanites. This was a fearless act of love and self-sacrifice. On more than one occasion their very lives were at stake. At the beginning of their service, as they prepared to separate and enter enemy territory, Alma reminded them of the importance and power of using the scriptures as their primary means of teaching and spiritual defense:

> And now, as the preaching of the word had a great tendency to lead the people to do that which was just—yea, it had had more powerful effect upon the minds of the people than the

> sword, or anything else, which had happened unto them—therefore Alma thought it was expedient that they should try the virtue of the word of God. (Alma 31:5)

These valiant missionaries soon learned the truth of Alma's counsel. They were attempting to reclaim a group of apostate Nephites who at one time had been taught the gospel. But because of disobedience and rebellion, they had fallen away and become hardened. "Neither would they observe the performances of the church, to continue in prayer and supplication to God daily, that they might not enter into temptation" (Alma 31:10). One of the consequences of this was that these Zoramites were now practicing a strange form of worship, "which Alma and his brethren had never beheld." One day each week, they would gather in their synagogue and then, one by one, climb to a high place and offer a set prayer, praising God for "electing" them to be His holy children.

Upon seeing this perversion of the truth, Alma and his brethren were heartsick. The story continues with their diligent efforts to bring some of these dissenters back into the true fold of God. The scriptures play a central role in their success among the "poor class of people," who after being cast out of the Zoramites' places of worship because of their poverty, come to Alma and Amulek and ask the poignant question, "What shall we do?" (Alma 32:5). This expression of sincere humility opens the door to conversion, and eventually many of the lost sheep are reclaimed.

In another Book of Mormon account, a group of Lamanites used the "power of the word" to change the hearts of a most unlikely audience. In the book of Helaman, we read the story of the Gadianton robbers, a secret combination of thieves and murderers who eventually caused the entire destruction of both the Jaredite and Nephite nations (see Ether 8:21). As Mormon relates the story, a group of converted Lamanites "did hunt the band of the robbers of Gadianton; *and they did preach the word of God among the more wicked part of them*, insomuch that this band of robbers was utterly destroyed from among the Lamanites" (Helaman 6:37; emphasis added). Lest we think that this is an isolated experience, modern-day prophets have repeatedly reminded us of the value of personal scripture study as it relates to spiritual healing.

President Ezra Taft Benson, in a landmark address entitled "The Power of the Word" given just prior to his first general conference as Church President, taught of the nourishing and healing virtue found only in the scriptures. Speaking to Church leaders, President Benson reminded them of the emotional help available through regular, prayerful scripture study:

> Do you have members in your stakes whose lives are shattered by sin or tragedy, who are in despair and without hope? Have you longed for some way to reach out and heal their wounds, soothe their troubled souls? The prophet Jacob offers just that with this remarkable promise: "They have come up hither to hear the pleasing word of God, yea, *the word which healeth the wounded soul.*" (Jacob 2:8; emphasis in original)

In spite of frequent prophetic reminders, many of us struggle to make the connection between regular scripture study and the resultant spiritual power that influences all of our other relationships and activities. For some reason we think that we can go it alone, even though our experiences affirm again and again that when we're separated from the True Vine, we can do nothing (see Moses 1:10; John 15:5; Philippians 4:13; Alma 26:12). Perhaps if we were to think of scripture study as a form of personal preparation for the daily battles we'll be required to fight, we might be more committed to making time for the word of the Lord. Understanding that the time spent nourishing our faith could directly impact the words we say and how we say them to a loved one.

Personal study qualifies us to have personal revelation in every aspect of our lives. Such personal devotion directly affects the outcomes of our parenting, family, work, and any other interactions. As President Benson reminded us,

> Success in righteousness, the power to avoid deception and resist temptation, guidance in our daily lives, healing of the soul—these are but a few of the promises the Lord has given to those who will come to His word. Does the Lord promise and not fulfill? Surely if He tells us that these things will come to us if we lay hold upon His word, then the blessings can be ours. And if we do not, then the blessings may be lost. However diligent we may be in other areas, certain blessings are to be found only in the scriptures, only in coming to the word of the Lord and holding fast to it as we make our way through the mists of darkness to the tree of life. ("The Power of the Word," *Ensign*, April 1986, 95)

For many years I struggled to lead my family in daily scripture study. There always seemed to be a good reason why we couldn't make the time for something we knew was important. Mornings seemed too hectic. Evenings often found us exhausted from the daily marathons in which we seemed to be regularly participating. Surely the Lord understood that we wanted to do it but that the timing just wasn't right—not right then. No doubt things would slow down soon and we would finally do what we knew we should.

Then one day it struck me. Although I wouldn't think of sending my children out the door unfed or inadequately dressed, I was regularly sending them out to face the challenges and temptations of the day with little or no spiritual food or armor to fortify and protect them. I knew I needed to repent and commit myself to make this practice a priority. Once I made this decision to lead my family in studying the scriptures together each day, somehow the time for doing so miraculously appeared. Even more important, the spirit in our home improved. Our children (and we as parents) got along better. We were kinder and more patient with each another. Problems at work and school and in church somehow seemed easier to solve. The solutions to those problems were more powerful and enduring.

President Marion G. Romney made the following promise to those who would make the practice of studying scriptures, especially the Book of Mormon, a central part of their lives:

> I feel certain that if, in our homes, parents will read from the Book of Mormon prayerfully and regularly, both by themselves and with their children, the spirit of that great book will come to permeate our homes and all who dwell therein. The spirit of reverence will increase; mutual respect and consideration for each other will grow. The spirit of contention will depart. Parents will counsel their children in greater love and wisdom. Children will be more responsive and submissive to the counsel of their parents. Righteousness will increase. Faith, hope, and charity—the pure love of Christ—will abound in our homes and lives, bringing in their wake peace, joy, and happiness. ("The Book of Mormon," *Ensign*, May 1980, 94).

What does all of this have to do with giving "beauty for ashes"? How does studying the scriptures relate to our becoming the Christlike response? In the scriptures we find the models, both good and bad, of how to live a Christlike life. In addition to the perfect model of the Savior, we read of the examples of ancient prophets such as Joseph, Abraham, Moses, Nephi, Alma, and Mormon, among many others. We see how they struggled with their own relationships and how, through the gospel, they became men and women of Christ.

> In the scriptures we find the models for how to live a Christlike life.

More important, in the scriptures we learn and are taught how to apply the doctrines of Christ, which are the simple, foundational principles of His gospel. As we regularly and prayerfully spend quality time immersed in the scriptures, we learn to recognize a singular Voice, calling out to us to "come, follow me." It is the voice of the Lord Jesus Christ. Of all the important truths that are available to the diligent seeker, none is as important as our becoming familiar with "the way, the truth, and the life." Coming to better know the Savior and His character as taught in the scriptures is the best reason for making time each day to quietly read and ponder.

Early in his ministry as an Apostle, Elder Spencer W. Kimball suffered several heart attacks within a span of two weeks. After spending almost two months recovering at home, he was anxious for a change of scenery. He made contact with old friends on the Navajo Indian reservation in New Mexico and arranged to spend some additional recuperation time among those he loved.

As recounted in the December 1985 *Ensign*, published at the time of President Kimball's death, one morning he was not in his bed. Attendants figured he had just taken a morning stroll and would be back for breakfast. But when he hadn't returned by 10 a.m., they started a search.

They finally found him under a pine tree several miles away. Next to him, his Bible lay open next to the last chapter of John. His eyes were closed, and he remained completely still as they approached him.

Their frightened voices aroused him, however, and when he lifted his head they could see traces of tears on his cheeks. When asked what he was doing, he replied, "Six years ago today I was called to be an Apostle of the Lord Jesus Christ, and I just wanted to spend the day with Him whose witness I am."

Just the chance that I might learn to become more like Him sends me thirsting for His words.

I never read this story without feeling that I am standing on holy ground. To imagine this humble, meek man of God, sitting under the quiet of a tree, seeking as an Apostle of Jesus Christ to know Him better, moves me to likewise desire to search the scriptures as I never have before. Even the possibility that I might learn how to become more like Him spurs me to come thirsting for His words. As the Savior Himself has said to all who will diligently seek Him,

> Draw near unto me and I will draw near unto you; seek me diligently and ye shall find

> me; ask, and ye shall receive; knock, and it shall be opened unto you. Whatsoever ye ask the Father in my name it shall be given unto you, that is expedient for you. . . . And if your eye be single to my glory, your whole bodies shall be filled with light, and there shall be no darkness in you; and that body which is filled with light comprehendeth all things. Therefore, sanctify yourselves that your minds become single to God, and the days will come that you shall see him; for he will unveil his face unto you, and it shall be in his own time, and in his own way, and according to his own will. (D&C 88:63–64, 67–68)

Developing a vibrant and deepening love for the scriptures is a task that is always in progress. This should be an invigorating thought to us and not one that discourages. The scriptures are a source of never-ending nourishment to the hungry, seeking soul. We have the privilege of coming unto Christ through our study of His words. This in turn brings about a quiet reformation of our hearts as we diligently strive to "liken all scripture" unto ourselves. This likening process is at the heart of the work of becoming the Christlike response. Experience readily confirms that such revolutionary work is not a one-time event but rather a steady, incremental movement in the right direction. As President Kimball taught,

> I am convinced that each of us, at least some time in our lives, must discover the scriptures for ourselves—and not just discover them once, but rediscover them again and again. . . .
>
> The Lord is not trifling with us when he gives us these things, for "unto whomsoever

> much is given, of him shall be much required." (Luke 12:48). Access to these things means responsibility for them. We must study the scriptures according to the Lord's commandment (see 3 Ne. 23:1–5); and we must let them govern our lives. (*Ensign,* Sept. 1976, 4–5)

Rather than treating our time spent in the scriptures as just one more task to be completed, if we instead think of scripture study as an essential part of the process of our becoming more like the Savior, we would likely be far more resolute in making sure we regularly "rediscover [the scriptures] again and again." Elder Bruce R. McConkie reminded us that some precious blessings come only to those that make this gospel habit a high priority:

> We are so wound up in programs and statistics and trends, in properties, lands and mammon, and in achieving goals that will highlight the excellence of our work, that we have "omitted the weightier matters of the law." . . . However talented men may be in administrative matters; however eloquent they may be in expressing their views; however learned they may be in the worldly things—they will be denied the sweet whisperings of the Spirit that might have been theirs unless they pay the price of studying, pondering, and praying about the scriptures. (In Regional Representatives' Seminar, 2 Apr. 1982, 1–2)

Certainly we've heard ample prophetic reminders of the importance of personal scripture study. We don't need more revelation to move us to act. We just need to act on counsel and revelation already received. As I learned in my struggle to lead my family in scripture study, the first step required was simply to decide that this activity was worth the effort required to make it happen. All of the blessings promised by President Romney have come to fruition in my family. Likewise, as I have exerted this same effort in my personal scripture study, I have seen the same or similar blessings fulfilled in my life. Interestingly, although it has gotten easier to make time for study each day, it still requires a daily recommitment to sustain these habits. This shouldn't be surprising. Just as we have the blessing of the sacrament each week to renew and remind us of baptismal covenants, we need to regularly retrench in order to keep our personal gospel practices alive.

> Real change is not for the faint of heart; setbacks and struggles are inevitable.

Most important, we must not give up. Establishing new patterns and breaking free of old ones is hard, challenging work. Real change is not for the faint of heart nor for the uncommitted. Setbacks and struggles are inevitable. As with so many other aspects of living the gospel, we are dependent on the Savior's grace and virtue to compensate for all of the ways in which we are lacking. He doesn't ask us to do anything that He isn't at the same time ready and able to help us do. This includes developing and nurturing the habit of personal scripture study.

In the moments when we are faltering and feel our resolve crumbling, He draws near and invites us to trust in Him. If we heed His loving words, we will find the strength needed to persevere. In our yearning to know Him, to follow Him, to become more like Him, the Bread of Life and the Living Waters found only in the scriptures are the necessary nutrients that will sustain us as we make our way forward. As Nephi and his family learned during their long journey in the wilderness, "We see that the commandments of God must be fulfilled. And if it so be that the children of men keep the commandments of God he doth nourish them, and strengthen them, and provide means whereby they can accomplish the thing which he has commanded them; wherefore, he did provide means for us while we did sojourn in the wilderness" (1 Nephi 17:3).

CHAPTER 9

"Unto such shall ye continue to minister." —3 Nephi 18:32

At this stage in our journey in becoming "beauty for ashes," we've hopefully discovered that the only path to our becoming more like the Savior is through choosing to access and then apply His grace and atoning power. We've been reminded that forgiveness is a central part of loving those who have offended us. We've reconnected our personal prayers and study of the scriptures to our soul-yearnings for at-one-ment with our Heavenly Father and with His Beloved Son, Jesus Christ. And we've been reminded that "loving our enemies" requires us not to take offense, even when someone's words and actions have been offensive.

All of these principles relate to the final part of our becoming "beauty for ashes." This step is a culmination of all of the other parts in this lifelong transformation. And it is the most daunting and at times even frightening part of the journey. It is the act of seeking out and ministering to those who have hurt or offended or even abused us. It is forgiveness in action. It is the essence of the Christlike response.

It is important to note at the beginning of this chapter that I am in no way suggesting that we put ourselves in harm's way, either spiritually, physically, or both. If we have been abused by a family member or by anyone else for that matter, the teachings of the Church are crystal clear in assuring us that our personal safety is of the highest priority to our leaders and to God. We should never think that forgiving someone who has brought us harm includes continuing to risk further hurt. Such thinking is false and should be firmly rejected. Any attempt by anyone to convince us that forgiveness includes our allowing the abuser to continue to be abusive is absolutely false. Forgiveness is vital to our spiritual health and ultimate spiritual attainment. But it must never be extended at the cost of our personal welfare and safety. The position of the Lord and His Church regarding abuse is summed up in two words: zero tolerance. Our position must be the same. If anyone reading these words has at any time been abused or is still under the threat of such treatment, I strongly urge you to seek help and safety right now.

Elder Richard G. Scott has spoken on several occasions about overcoming the destructive effects of abuse. In at least two different talks given during general conference, he has counseled both the victims and the perpetrators of abuse that there is hope and available healing to those who seek these blessings. At the same time, he has always been quick to remind those being abused that they are not at fault and that they must first ensure that any form of abuse must not be allowed to continue:

> If you are currently being abused or have been in the past, find the courage to seek help. You may have been severely threatened or caused to fear so that you would not reveal the abuse. Have the courage to act now. Seek the support of someone you can trust. Your bishop or stake

> president can give you valuable counsel and help you with the civil authorities. Explain how you have been abused and identify who has done it. Ask for protection. Your action may help others avoid becoming innocent victims, with the consequent suffering. Get help now. Do not fear—for fear is a tool Satan will use to keep you suffering. The Lord will help you, but you must reach out for that help. ("To Heal the Shattering Consequences of Abuse," *Ensign*, April 2008, 42)

Both of the talks he's given on this topic should be read in their entirety. The first one is entitled "Healing the Tragic Scars of Abuse" and was given in the April 1992 general conference. Sixteen years later, during the April 2008 general conference, Elder Scott spoke again on this topic in an address entitled "To Heal the Shattering Consequences of Abuse." Many other examples could be cited that make it clear that there is no tolerance of abuse in any form, either by the Lord Himself or by His Church.

With this understanding in place, I proceed with some thoughts on the importance of seeking out those who have hurt or offended us, in hopes of reconciliation. Isaiah refers to those who seek out others as "repairers of the breach" (Isaiah 58:12). In His counsel to His disciples in the Book of Mormon, the Savior Himself spoke of the importance of continuing our outreach to those with whom we may be at odds. After speaking of those who may not be worthy to partake of all the blessings of Church membership, the Lord reminds us, "Nevertheless, ye shall not cast him out of your synagogues, or your places of worship, *for unto such shall ye continue to minister*; for ye know not but what they will return and repent, and come unto me with full purpose of heart, and I shall heal them; and ye shall be the means of bringing salvation unto them" (3 Nephi 18:32; emphasis added).

Just how do we "continue to minister"? What does such ministering look like? What if the person we are ministering to wants no part of such outreach? Such questions are best answered by seeking for and obtaining personal revelation, with the understanding that we are not in a position to receive revelation for others unless we have familial or ecclesiastical authority to do so. But we can counsel with the Lord to obtain guidance in our efforts to show offended or offending brothers or sisters that we love them and want them to know they are forgiven. Such ministry is independent of any calling or assignment.

A brief story shared by Sister Bonnie D. Parkin captures the spirit of this ministry. It doesn't involve any offended parties but rather an attempt by someone to give a gift to someone loved and admired, even when she was unsure of the value of her offering:

> My daughter-in-law's mother, Susan, was a wonderful seamstress. President [Spencer W.] Kimball lived in their ward. One Sunday, Susan noticed that he had a new suit. Her father had recently returned from a trip to New York and had brought her some exquisite silk fabric. Susan thought that fabric would make a handsome tie to go with President Kimball's new suit. So on Monday she made the tie. She wrapped it in tissue paper and walked up the block to President Kimball's home.
>
> On her way to the front door, she suddenly stopped and thought, "Who am I to make a tie for the prophet? He probably has plenty of them." Deciding she had made a mistake, she turned to leave.

> Just then Sister Kimball opened the front door and said, "Oh, Susan!"
>
> Stumbling all over herself, Susan said, "I saw President Kimball in his new suit on Sunday. Dad just brought me some silk from New York . . . and so I made him a tie."
>
> Before Susan could continue, Sister Kimball stopped her, took hold of her shoulders, and said: "Susan, never suppress a generous thought." ("Personal Ministry," *BYU Speeches*, February 13, 2007)

This story beautifully illustrates the essence of what I hope to share in this chapter on the importance of continuing to minister, even to those who appear to have no interest in such efforts. In one sense, how someone chooses to respond to our attempts at ministering doesn't matter. Agency is an essential part of mortality. How we choose to exercise our agency is the purpose of mortality. This is true even when our agency is exercised unwisely. Even so, any effort made to be "at one" with a brother offended is a reflection of this counsel from Sister Kimball to "never suppress a generous thought" and can only lead to healing, even if that healing is restricted to our own hearts.

Because this is a book about our becoming the Christlike response, it's important to discuss how "continuing to minister" relates to this core principle. A verse in the Book of Mormon refers to Nephi, the prophet who was present during the ministry of the Savior to the Nephites, and illustrates how our personal discipleship can influence others, even those who may be considered our "enemies." In discussing how Nephi went about teaching and ministering to the people, the account mentions those who were offended by his efforts: "And it came to pass that they were angry with him, even because he had greater power than they, *for it were not possible that they could disbelieve his words*, for so great was his faith on the Lord Jesus Christ that angels did minister unto him daily" (3 Nephi 7:18; emphasis added).

Talk about spiritual power! Nephi's faith and righteousness was so authentic and influential that even those who didn't want to believe him could not doubt his words. Earlier we learn the source of Nephi's great influential authority. During the difficult days just prior to the Savior's appearance in the Americas, Nephi is faced with rising rebellion both in the government and within the Church itself. He attempts to persuade the people to repent but seems to fail in his efforts to do so. As he returns to his home, pondering over the moral collapse of those once firm in the faith,

> Behold, a voice came unto him saying: Blessed art thou, Nephi, for those things which thou hast done; for I have beheld how thou hast with unwearyingness declared the word, which I have given unto thee, unto this people. And thou hast not feared them, and hast not sought thine own life, but hast sought my will, and to keep my commandments.
>
> And now, because thou hast done this with such unwearyingness, behold, I will bless thee forever; and I will make thee mighty in word and in deed, in faith and in works; yea, even that all things shall be done unto thee according to thy word, for thou shalt not ask that which is contrary to my will.
>
> Behold, thou art Nephi, and I am God. Behold, I declare it unto thee in the presence of mine angels, that ye shall have power over this people, and shall smite the earth with famine,

> and with pestilence, and destruction, according to the wickedness of this people.
>
> Behold, I give unto you power, that whatsoever ye shall seal on earth shall be sealed in heaven; and whatsoever ye shall loose on earth shall be loosed in heaven; and thus shall ye have power among this people. (Helaman 10:3–5)

The source of Nephi's ability to influence and change the hearts of those opposed to him was, of course, the Lord Jesus Christ. Just as the Savior told Nephi that "all things shall be done unto thee according to thy word," we too can receive this same remarkable promise from Him. There is no limit to the reach of such influence, just as there is no limit to the power of the Atonement to heal and to restore and to repair the breach between estranged parties.

Elder F. Enzio Busche shared a wonderful example of this in a talk he gave at BYU–Idaho in 2005 entitled "The Joy We Are All Waiting For." In a beautiful way it illustrates how Jesus Christ, if invited, can shape us into instruments of influence, even to the transforming of our relationships from sharp estrangement into joyous at-one-ment.

During his first years of membership in the Church, the branch was so small and the members so inexperienced that the missionaries were serving as branch presidents. Not everyone felt comfortable approaching these young missionaries with their personal questions.

One day a thirty-year-old woman approached Elder Busche about her difficulty in finding a spouse who matched her. As part of her question, she asked what he thought the purpose of her life might be. He struggled to answer her question.

Just a few weeks later, he and his wife were very surprised to receive from her a wedding announcement. Her husband-to-be was a member of the branch and was hardly her match:

he was about ten years younger than she, had hardly any formal education, and was nearly a head shorter than she.

A little more than a year later, Elder Busche was serving as the branch president when once again this woman wanted to have a private conversation. The moment the door closed, she started complaining about all the things she didn't like about her husband—his lack of table manners, his bad breath, his clumsy way of speaking, and on and on.

When Elder Busche asked if she remembered their conversation from a year earlier, she responded that she did. He suggested that maybe her purpose in life was to help bring this young man to the celestial kingdom. She reacted as if she had been hit with a whip. Without saying another word, she left the room.

As he told it:

> Many years later, much more than a generation after I had my talk with this sister, I was with Sister Busche visiting in Germany to preside over a stake conference. I was sitting on the stand and I was impressed with the large audience filling that spacious stake center to the last seat. Suddenly my eyes became glued to a nice elderly couple with an overwhelming glow of happiness and joy on their faces. He was holding her hand in one hand and gently, lovingly touching her hand with his other hand. On the left and on the right of them I could see children and grandchildren, as it was not difficult to recognize them by their resemblance. Then, when I noticed that he was much smaller than she, it suddenly struck me: my goodness, I know these people. And the full memory of my talk with this gentle lady from so many years ago came

> into my mind. My heart was rejoicing with the impressive awareness: SHE DID IT! SHE DID IT! Now I could see that she had made the sacrifice, that she had paid the price; she had overcome the natural man inside of her, and had obviously learned to love him without conditions. He had grown to become that impressive, gray-haired gentleman with aristocratic demeanor, and bliss radiating from his countenance, a radiation that can only be felt from someone who has learned to know God. And it was easy to see that now she would not give him up for anything. ("The Joy We Are All Waiting For," BYU–Idaho, February 2005)

This wonderful story provides a perfect summary of giving "beauty for ashes." It shows us in a poignant way how hard such a process can be (and sometimes how long!) but also expresses the life-changing power of such Christlike decisions. This good sister chose. She chose to see her husband not as he was but as the Lord knew he could become. In so doing she became as well. With the encouragement of a loving priesthood leader, she sought for spiritual vision to stretch beyond her own limited sight. As Elder Busche witnessed, "She had made the sacrifice . . . she had paid the price; she had overcome the natural man inside of her, and had obviously learned to love him without conditions."

In our own faltering efforts to give "beauty for ashes," there will always be opposition. This shouldn't surprise us, knowing as we do that the foundation of God's plan is moral agency. As Lehi taught in his discourse on the subject, "For it must needs be, that there is an opposition in all things. If not so . . . righteousness could not be brought to pass, neither wickedness, neither holiness nor misery, neither good nor bad

. . . Wherefore, the Lord God gave unto man that he should act for himself. Wherefore, man could not act for himself save it should be that he was enticed by the one or the other" (2 Nephi 2:11, 16).

Opposition comes in countless forms. But come it surely will, and in some cases repeatedly. This also should not be surprising to us. Moroni shared this important idea in his discussion of faith in the book of Ether. "I would show unto the world that faith is things which are hoped for and not seen; wherefore, dispute not because ye see not, *for ye receive no witness until after the trial of your faith*" (Ether 12:6; emphasis added). The purpose of all mortal testing is to see what we will choose when faced with the reality of choice. Elder Neal A. Maxwell poignantly reflected on the sobering consequences of our having chosen God's plan:

> I'm not sure we grasp how the final judgment will reflect our choices! But my desires and choices really will be honored! How manifestly just of God! How trembling for me! There is the anxiety protruding once again. Are my desires sufficiently educated to choose wisely (see Alma 13:3, 10)? Could the further education of my desires be the most important form of continuing education?
>
> So it is that the chilly dawn of realization is further felt: Real choosing bristles with alternatives, enticements, defining moments, accountability, counterfeits, and consequences! ("Free to Choose?" *BYU Speeches*, March 16, 2004)

In some instances, our strivings to reach out to rescue may include real risk of emotional or even physical harm. While we certainly shouldn't seek for such circumstances, at times they are unavoidable. In these moments, the depth of our "mighty change of heart" is truly tested. In a story first broadcast on National Public Radio in 2008, a young man named Julio Diaz recounted an experience he had with a mugger in a New York subway station. His daily routine each night included stopping one stop early in order to eat at his favorite diner in the Bronx. One evening as he stepped off the train onto the nearly empty platform, he was approached by a teenage boy who pulled out a knife.

> He wants my money, so I just gave him my wallet and told him, "Here you go," Diaz says.
>
> As the teen began to walk away, Diaz told him, "Hey, wait a minute. You forgot something. If you're going to be robbing people for the rest of the night, you might as well take my coat to keep you warm."
>
> The would-be robber looked at his would-be victim, "like what's going on here?" Diaz says. "He asked me, 'Why are you doing this?'"
>
> Diaz responded that it was clear the young man must have a need and that if that was true, perhaps he could join him for dinner.
>
> Diaz says he and the teen went into the diner and sat in a booth.
>
> "The manager comes by, the dishwashers come by, the waiters come by to say hi," Diaz says. "The kid was like, 'You know everybody here. Do you own this place?'"
>
> "No, I just eat here a lot," Diaz says he told the teen. "He says, 'But you're even nice to the dishwasher.'"
>
> Diaz replied, "Well, haven't you been taught you should be nice to everybody?"

> "Yea, but I didn't think people actually behaved that way," the teen said. . . .
>
> When the bill arrived, Diaz told the teen, "Look, I guess you're going to have to pay for this bill cause you have my money and I can't pay for this. So if you give me my wallet back, I'll gladly treat you."
>
> The teen "didn't even think about it" and returned the wallet, Diaz says. "I gave him $20 . . . I figure maybe it'll help him. I don't know."
>
> Diaz says he asked for something in return—the teen's knife—"and he gave it to me."
>
> Afterward, when Diaz told his mother what happened, she said, "You're the type of kid that if someone asked you for the time, you gave them your watch."
>
> "I figure, you know, if you treat people right, you can only hope that they treat you right. It's as simple as it gets in this complicated world." ("A Victim Treats His Mugger Right," NPR, March 28, 2008)

Notice how affected this young man was by the kindness shown to him and how quick he was to return Mr. Diaz's wallet, followed by his own weapon. Clearly he was confused by the way he was treated, which was undeserved. Was his heart changed? At least for this brief moment in a subway diner, yes. All of the violence and animosity in his heart was removed, and he became humble and submissive. Something deep in his heart was stirred by the "beauty for ashes" given to him by Mr. Diaz. It's likely that he has never forgotten that night. Of course, we would hope that the spirit of that moment lingered in his mind and perhaps even changed the course of his life. Such is the power of exchanging good for evil. However, even if a gift is rejected, the one offering is better for having made the attempt. And as the account of Nephi reminds us, even those rejecting our attempts at ministering can't help but be influenced by the spirit of the offering. Even if it takes years or even decades to result in change, such efforts are never wasted.

Robert and Ann Daines learned this truth firsthand as they attempted to raise their family in New Jersey during a time when the Church was a tiny minority. Just after buying a house in what appeared to be a welcoming neighborhood, they received some unwelcomed news. A Latter-day Saint family who had lived nearby warned them that after their baptism, they had to move from the neighborhood because of anti-Mormon sentiment. This family pleaded with the Daineses not to move into the neighborhood.

But they had already signed a contract, so they moved into the house. At first, things seemed to be going okay. The neighbors were nice and the children seemed to be accepted. But after a little time had gone by, they noticed that while children came to their home to play, their own children were never invited to play at other homes.

Robert and Anna discussed the problem for quite a while. They could move but knew it would be difficult to find another home because of housing shortages. That's not all—they didn't want to run away. So they decided to try to change the community's attitude toward the Church.

Over the course of the next several months, they made great sacrifices in order to serve in their community, both getting involved on boards and committees. Gradually, they began making a big difference as people accepted them and saw the contributions they were making:

> At the end of her first three-year term on the YMCA board, Anna Daines was reelected. Two terms are the most any board member can

> serve, and a man who had served that amount of time was leaving. They had a farewell dinner for him. After the dinner, this man took Sister Daines aside and said, "I must tell you before I leave that I was the one who spearheaded the campaign not to let the Mormons use this hall. I didn't know anything good about the Mormons; I had never known a Mormon. But from the things I'd heard about them, I didn't want to know any.
>
> "I feel that I owe you an apology," he said. "After seeing what fine people you are, I'm embarrassed to think that I did that."

Brother Daines had a similar experience in his role as a member of the local school board. During a heated debate over whether the school districts should be combined and where a baccalaureate service should be held, he was able to restore calm and spearhead a solution that everyone accepted.

He called a meeting of all the town's ministers:

> At the start he announced that because it was a school meeting, he would preside. The minister of the leading church didn't like that much—he didn't think it was right for a layman to preside over the clergy. But Brother Daines insisted—and he called on himself to open with prayer!
>
> He prayed that everyone there would put the interests of the community first, "that we would be big enough to do the things that were best for all the youth."
>
> And there was a spirit of harmony—not a dissenting voice in the whole meeting.
>
> At the baccalaureate service in the school gym, all the churches were represented. As

> a Latter-day Saint, Brother Daines gave the opening prayer. The monsignor of the Catholic Church gave the address. The minister of the Black congregation had a part, as did the Jewish rabbi and the various Protestant ministers. And despite the deep feelings that the change caused at first, this has been the pattern ever since. (Orson Scott Card, "Neighborliness: Daines Style," *Ensign*, Apr. 1977, 19)

The story of Ammon's mission to the Lamanites in the Book of Mormon provides a similar model of how powerful one's influence can be, even when faced with a long-standing enemy. After Ammon had preserved the flocks of King Lamoni, instead of returning to the king to boast of his "disarming" personality, he instead sought for new ways to serve him. When the king asked his servants, "Where is this man that has such great power?" they replied that he was feeding the king's horses. "Now when king Lamoni heard that Ammon was preparing his horses and chariots he was more astonished, because of the faithfulness of Ammon, saying: Surely there has not been any servant among all my servants that has been so faithful as this man; for even he doth remember all my commandments to execute them" (Alma 18:9–10).

The king was so affected by Ammon's selflessness that he couldn't even speak to him when Ammon came to report that he'd finished his responsibilities. For an hour Ammon waited for the king to speak, discerning through the Spirit that the king desired to know by what power he was able to perform such great miracles. The king's heart was undergoing a mighty change, even though Ammon hadn't yet spoken a single word of doctrine in his presence. Ammon had lived the doctrine, and the power of that had moved the king to desire to give Ammon whatever he asked for. Once his heart was prepared, "Ammon began to speak unto him with boldness, and said unto him: Believest thou that there is a God?" (Alma 18:24). Ammon proceeded to teach the king the doctrine of Christ, which would eventually lead to the conversion of many Lamanites.

> And they did all declare unto the people the self-same thing—that their hearts had been changed; that they had no more desire to do evil. . . .
>
> And it came to pass that there were many that did believe in their words; and as many as did believe were baptized; and they became a righteous people, and they did establish a church among them.
>
> And thus the work of the Lord did commence among the Lamanites; thus the Lord did begin to pour out his Spirit upon them; and we see that his arm is extended to all people who will repent and believe in his name. (Alma 19:33, 35–36)

After this miraculous series of events, Ammon and King Lamoni left to save Ammon's missionary companions, who had been taken prisoner in the land of Middoni. Because of the experiences leading to king Lamoni's conversion, he didn't attend the great feast hosted by Lamoni's father, the king of all the Lamanites. His father set out to learn why Lamoni was absent, and met his son along with Ammon on the way to the land of Middoni. After asking Lamoni why he hadn't come to the great feast, he confronted his son by asking "Whither art thou going with this Nephite, who is one of the children of a liar?" (Alma 20:10).

Lamoni's father tried to persuade him to slay Ammon and was stunned to hear that his son not only refused to do so but also then added insult to injury by testifying that he knew "they are just men and holy prophets of the true God" (Alma 20:15). Irate, Lamoni's father drew his sword to slay his son. Ammon first rebuked and then easily disarmed him. Lamoni's father pleaded for his life, offering half of his kingdom if Ammon would refrain from slaying him. Ammon asked only that his brethren be released from prison and that Lamoni be allowed to retain his kingdom and newfound faith:

> Now when Ammon had said these words, the king began to rejoice because of his life.
>
> And when he saw that Ammon had no desire to destroy him, and when he also saw the great love he had for his son Lamoni, he was astonished exceedingly, and said: Because this is all that thou hast desired, that I would release thy brethren, and suffer that my son Lamoni should retain his kingdom, behold, I will grant unto you that my son may retain his kingdom from this time and forever; and I will govern him no more—
>
> And I will also grant unto thee that thy brethren may be cast out of prison, and thou and thy brethren may come unto me, in my kingdom; for I shall greatly desire to see thee. For the king was greatly astonished at the words which he had spoken, and also at the words which had been spoken by his son Lamoni, therefore he was desirous to learn them. (Alma 20:25–27)

As before, Ammon taught true doctrine simply by living true doctrine. Without teaching Lamoni's father a single gospel principle, he invited the power of true doctrine into the king's heart through the power of his example. Soon after this experience, the king of the Lamanites would also accept the gospel message and be converted and baptized, all because of the spiritual influence of a humble servant of God.

In our own efforts to minister to those from whom we are estranged, motive is an important determining factor in how much effect our efforts will have. If we are seeking to get even or to score points, then any possibility of touching the heart of a brother or sister is unlikely. In fact, if our motives are selfish or vengeful, it's likely that we'll do more harm than good to those we're trying to reach. Certainly it is not easy to have pure motives, nor is it required that our motivation be wholly Christlike before we make any effort to rescue one we love. Earnest prayer and at times even the spirit of fasting may be needed in order to bring about a sufficient change in our hearts.

> If our motives are selfish or vengeful, it's likely we'll do more harm than good to those we're trying to reach.

Often this change comes during our rescue efforts. It is as if the Lord is acknowledging our imperfect attempts to do the right thing, even when we are so imperfect in how we go about doing it. As discussed earlier, this is where His atoning grace becomes an "enabling power," compensating as it does for all the many ways in which we may yet lack. The Savior can and is always willing to make up the vast difference between our intentions and our actions. He can also help us to change our motives so that they are in harmony with His perfect priorities. If we yearn to be reconciled with someone, we can call upon our Father in prayer and ask for His help in purifying our desires so that they are righteous and not vindictive.

In speaking of our desire to influence the lost sheep, I recognize that I speak of tender things. In particular, if our words or actions were at least part of the reason for someone turning away from the gospel path, we feel, as did the sons of Mosiah in the Book of Mormon, "That perhaps [we] might bring them to the knowledge of the Lord their God, and convince them of the iniquity of their fathers; and that perhaps they might cure them of their hatred . . . that they might also be brought to rejoice in the Lord their God, that they might become friendly to one another, and that there should be no more contentions. . . . Now they were desirous that salvation should be declared to every creature, for they could not bear that any human soul should perish; yea, even the very thoughts that any soul should endure endless torment did cause them to quake and tremble" (Mosiah 28:2–3).

We too may tremble at the thought of losing a brother or sister, and our hearts likewise will be drawn out in "long strugglings" for our brethren to be restored to full fellowship. The Savior's gentle admonition to "continue to minister" is an open-ended one. In the timing of heaven, it may take years or even decades before those we have lost will be found again. With trust in the Lord we simply continue to invite, to express love, and to prayerfully seek for ways to bind up wounds long since replaced by scars. "For ye know not but what they will return and repent, and come unto me with full purpose of heart, and I shall heal them; and ye shall be the means of bringing salvation unto them" (3 Nephi 18:32).

Elder Boyd K. Packer shared an experience he had at a stake conference that confirmed the importance of inviting those whom some may not consider "worthy" to come back.

Several years earlier he had visited a stake that was presided over by a man of unusual efficiency and ability. Every detail had been attended to, and there was a detailed agenda. Elder

Packer noticed that there was a twenty-minute period in one session that had not been scheduled, and he told the stake president they should call on some to speak who might need the "strengthening experience."

Near the close of the meeting, the stake president mentioned that he kept thinking of the mayor but whispered that the man was not active in the Church. Elder Packer suggested that the mayor be invited to speak anyway; though the stake president continued to resist, he finally invited the mayor at Elder Packer's insistence.

What happened was remarkable. In Elder Packer's words:

> The mayor's father had been a pioneer of the Church in that region. He had served as bishop of one of the wards and had been succeeded by one of his sons—a twin to the mayor, as I recall. The mayor was the lost sheep. He came to the pulpit and spoke, to my surprise, with bitterness and with hostility. His talk began something like this: "I don't know why you called on me. I don't know why I am in church today. I don't belong in church. I have never fit in. I don't agree with the way the Church does things."
>
> Then he just melted. "I know the gospel is true," he said. "I've always known it was true. I learned that from my mother as a boy.
>
> "I know the Church isn't out of order," he confessed. "It's me that's out of order, and I've always known that too."
>
> Then he spoke perhaps for all of the lost sheep when he pleaded: "I know it's me that is wrong, and I want to come back. I have been trying to come back, but you won't let me!"
>
> Of course we would let him come back,

> but somehow we hadn't let him know that. After the meeting the congregation flooded up—not to us but to him to say, "Welcome home!"

Helping the Savior reclaim His lost sheep is soul-stretching work. It is never easy. Patience and vision are always required. The attribute of charity, the "pure love of Christ," is always a key to our success. In Mormon's efforts to remind us of this, he teaches that long-suffering is a central characteristic of loving and rescuing others:

> Helping the Savior reclaim His lost sheep is soul-stretching work. It is never easy. Patience and vision are always required.

"And charity suffereth long, and is kind, and envieth not, and is not puffed up, seeketh not her own, is not easily provoked, thinketh no evil, and rejoiceth not in iniquity but rejoiceth in the truth, beareth all things, believeth all things, hopeth all things, endureth all things" (Moroni 7:45). In order for us to have influence for good on disaffected brothers or sisters, they must feel that we love them without conditions or expectations. Our motives must be pure, and charity is the Lord's way of purifying our hearts.

Joseph Smith taught early members of the Church that their ability to reach those they loved would be directly related to how they viewed those they were attempting to rescue:

> Don't be limited in your views with regard to your neighbors' virtues. . . . You must enlarge your souls toward others if you'd do like Jesus. . . . As you increase in innocence and virtue, as you increase in goodness, let your hearts expand—let them be enlarged towards others—you must be longsuffering and bear with the faults and errors of mankind. How precious are the souls of men!" (*Relief Society Minute Book* [Nauvoo, Illinois, Apr. 28, 1842], 39)

In the parable of the prodigal son, we are taught the importance of "continuing to minister" to those we love, even if it may seem as if there is no hope of ever rescuing the lost sheep. Often the "prodigals" must suffer at least some of the painful consequences of their choices before they will come to themselves (see Luke 15:17). Only then are their hearts sufficiently softened and prepared for healing. But as the father in the parable shows us, we must ever be working, watching, and praying for the prodigal's return.

The poignant moment of the prodigal son's return is one of the most powerful in all literature:

> And he arose, and came to his father. *But when he was yet a great way off, his father saw him*, and had compassion, and ran, and fell on his neck, and kissed him.
>
> And the son said unto him, Father, I have sinned against heaven, and in thy sight, and am no more worthy to be called thy son.
>
> But the father said to his servants, Bring forth the best robe, and put it on him; and put a ring on his hand, and shoes on his feet:

> And bring the fatted calf, and kill it; and let us eat, and be merry:
>
> For this my son was dead, and is alive again; he was lost, and is found. (Luke 15:20–24; emphasis added)

This son had squandered the inheritance given to him by a loving father. Instead of returning the love of his parents, he had turned his back on them, choosing instead to defile his covenants with "riotous living." After a famine arose (which always eventually happens), he found himself competing with swine for slop. He then resolved to return home, hoping only for the opportunity to be a hired servant, considering himself no longer worthy of his father's love or good name. But his father did as we each must do if we are to be disciples of Jesus Christ. He willingly, fully, and unconditionally forgave his son and showed this through the significant gifts he bestowed on his once-errant lamb. Perhaps most important, he had ever been on the lookout for his son's return, as noted in the meaningful phrase, "But when he was yet a great way off, his father saw him."

CHAPTER 10

"My grace is sufficient for all men." —Ether 12:27

WE BEGAN OUR JOURNEY TOWARD becoming "beauty for ashes" with the account of the Savior entering a garden on the night prior to His being mocked, beaten, spit on, and ultimately crucified. In that garden we know He took upon Himself the sins of the world. Through modern revelation we also know that He suffered the sum of all human weakness, sin, inadequacy, illness, pain, loneliness, and grief. In a way we cannot comprehend, He took upon Himself everything for everyone. Every mistake ever made. Every offense ever committed. Every wound, every hurt, every imperfection.

Truly He did as He had promised on that day, three years previous in the temple, when He proclaimed to all present, and to us, that

> The Spirit of the Lord God is upon me; because the Lord hath anointed me to preach good tidings unto the meek; he hath sent me to bind up the brokenhearted, to proclaim liberty

> to the captives, and the opening of the prison to them that are bound;
>
> To proclaim the acceptable year of the Lord, and the day of vengeance of our God; to comfort all that mourn;
>
> To appoint unto them that mourn in Zion, *to give unto them beauty for ashes*, the oil of joy for mourning, the garment of praise for the spirit of heaviness; that they might be called trees of righteousness, the planting of the Lord, that he might be glorified. (Isaiah 61:1–3; emphasis added)

In that quiet garden and later on the cruel cross, He finished the work He had been given to do. He had indeed bound up the brokenhearted, comforted all that mourned, provided the garment of praise for the spirit of heaviness—and again and again, in every moment of His ministry, He had given beauty for ashes. Indeed, He was beauty for ashes. No matter the form and intensity of our "ashes," Jesus Christ is able to transform them into something beautiful. If we are in fact His "work and glory" (Moses 1:39), then it should not surprise us that He is eager to help us become even as He is. We are what He lives for, just as we are what He died for.

In our personal, imperfect efforts to become more like the Savior, we can take great hope in His many promises to help us. We should never think we must do it on our own. Our personal efforts will always and ever be insufficient, for as Nephi taught, "We are saved by grace after all we can do." The "all we can do" part of that equation makes up a tiny fraction of what is ultimately required for us to be perfected. And that perfecting process is an eternal one, extending far beyond our brief moment on the mortal stage. But of the many tests that make up mortality, how we respond to the ones that occur in our human interactions and relationships will largely determine our happiness in the life to come. Thus it is crucial that we commit ourselves to the ongoing process of becoming "even as [He] is."

In our efforts to become more like the Savior, we can take great hope in His many promises to help us.

As we read about the life of the Savior, we are continually reminded that His every choice, every thought, and every action were other-centered. As He taught His disciples, "For I came down from heaven, not to do mine own will, but the will of him that sent me" (John 6:38). This singular characteristic defined every moment of the Lord's mortal ministry. "And he that sent me is with me: the Father hath not left me alone; *for I do always those things that please him*" (John 8:29; emphasis added). Though by design our fallen natures prevent us from escaping the effects of sin and selfishness, we can strive through the Atonement to "do always" those things that please heaven. The Savior has and will show us the way.

Nowhere is this more true than was shown in the last week of His life. In spite of intense personal suffering and indescribable spiritual anguish, the Savior continued to "give beauty for ashes," just as He had done through every waking moment of His mortal mission. As a beautiful Latter-day Saint hymn reminds us, "He marked the path, and led the way" ("How Great the Wisdom and the Love," *Hymns*, no. 195). Beginning with His Triumphal Entry into Jerusalem and concluding with His ignominious death on Calvary's lonely hill, the final hours of the Savior's life were filled with loving acts, both universal and singular. Even though "He was despised and rejected of men; a man of sorrows, and acquainted with grief" (Isaiah 53:3), he showed us how to endure in love and loving kindness to the end.

Among the many examples that could be cited, the following are representative of the Savior's selflessness during the hours and moments leading up to His greatest example of "giving beauty for ashes": His Atonement, Crucifixion, and Resurrection. Knowing that His death was imminent, the Savior instructed His disciples to prepare for the Passover by finding the upper room that had been prepared for just this moment. In spite of the celebratory mood surrounding the feast of unleavened bread, the Lord's mood was somber. Not only was He facing the awful hours in Gethsemane and on the cross, but He also knew of Judas's betrayal and sorrowed over the treachery of one of His special witnesses.

During the Last Supper, two scenes in particular personify the Savior's ever-constant kindness and concern for others—even for those who would do Him harm. Of the four recorded accounts of the Last Supper, only John recounts the story of the Savior washing the feet of His disciples—including those of Judas. After partaking of the traditional Passover meal, which included eating the firstborn lamb and unleavened bread, both rich with symbolism of what was to occur that very night, the Savior then proceeded to administer the ordinance of the washing of feet. In his book *The Life of Christ*, Frederic W. Farrar writes of this scene and of its significance:

> Every Eastern room, if it belongs to any but the very poorest, has the central part of the floor covered with mats, and as a person enters, he lays aside his sandals at the door of the room, mainly in order not to defile the clean

white mats with the dust and dirt of the road or streets, and also (at any rate among Mohammedans) because the mat is hallowed by being knelt upon in prayer. Before they reclined at the table, the disciples had doubtless conformed to this cleanly and reasonable custom; but another customary and pleasant habit, which we know that Jesus appreciated, had been neglected. Their feet must have been covered with dust from their walk along the hot and much frequented road from Bethany to Jerusalem, and under such circumstances they would have been refreshed for the festival by washing their feet after putting off their sandals.

But to wash the feet was the work of slaves; and since no one had offered to perform the kindly office, Jesus Himself, in His eternal humility and self-denial, rose from His place at the meal to do the menial service which none of His disciples had offered to do for Him. Well may the amazement of the beloved disciple show itself in his narrative, as he dwells on every particular of that solemn scene. Though He knew that the Father had given all things into His hands, and that He came from God and was going to God, He arose from the supper and laid aside His garments, and taking a towel, girded Himself." It is probable that in the utterness of self-abnegation. He entirely stripped His upper limbs, laying aside both the simchah and the cetoneth as though He had been the meanest slave, and wrapping the towel round His waist. Then pouring water into the large copper bason with which an Oriental house is always provided, He

> began without a word to wash His disciples' feet, and wipe them dry with the towel which served Him as a girdle. (New York: E. F. Dutton, 1875, 375)

The humility shown here by the Savior is representative of how He spent His entire life, as Peter had said, going about "doing good" (Acts 10:38). With the events of the evening and the next day no doubt weighing heavily upon Him, He still sought to serve. Of all those present in the room, He was the one most in need of service, yet He abased Himself and showed His disciples in all ages that to be the greatest is to be "the least and the servant of all" (D&C 50:26). As the Savior reminded them,

> Ye call me Master and Lord: and ye say well; for so I am.
>
> If I then, your Lord and Master, have washed your feet; ye also ought to wash one another's feet.
>
> For I have given you an example, that ye should do as I have done to you.
>
> Verily, verily, I say unto you, The servant is not greater than his lord, neither he that is sent greater than he that sent him.
>
> If you know these things, happy are ye if ye do them. (John 13:13–17)

That the Lord gave of Himself in this way is, in and of itself, an expression of profound love. But that He included Judas in this sacred ordinance is almost beyond comprehension. The Savior knew fully concerning His Apostle's betrayal. And yet He tried—even up to the moment when Judas left the presence of the Light of the World to commit the darkest of deeds—to provide a way for this man whom He loved to choose another way. But it was not to be. Judas was so bold as to mockingly ask, "Master, is it I?" in reply to the Savior's sorrowful pronouncement that one of those present in the room would betray Him. Even so, Jesus included Judas in the tender moment of washing of feet, providing him one final opportunity to turn back from the precipice he was nearing.

When one we love offends or even betrays us, we can look to the example of Jesus when choosing how to respond.

In a much lesser but still important way, we too will face moments in life when we are "deserving" of service. We too will be faced with the challenge of whether to be the one being washed instead of the one doing the washing. At the end of yet another long day, when we would like nothing better than to sit in front of the television with a bowl of ice cream while someone else takes care of dirty dishes and tired children, we can look to the Savior for "a more excellent way." And when someone we love offends or even betrays us, we likewise can look to the example of Jesus when choosing how to respond to the unfair way we've been treated. None of these choices is easy. Choosing to respond in a Christlike way to all of our mortal tests is the supreme measurement of true greatness. As President Ezra Taft Benson taught, "Christ is our ideal. He is our exemplar. What manner of men and women should we be? Even as He is (see 3 Ne. 27:27). The best measure of true greatness is how Christlike we are" ("A Sacred Responsibility," *Ensign*, May 1986).

As this most important night in the history of the world proceeded, Jesus showed us again and again "the way, the truth, and the life" (John 14:6). At the conclusion of the meal and after Judas had departed into the gloomy darkness of treachery, the Lord continued to bless and comfort and instruct. Whether in the moment of gentle rebuke and prophetic warning to Peter, who later that same night would thrice deny that he knew Jesus, or the moving moment when He restored the ear of Malchus after it was severed by a still impulsive Peter, Christ showed us the way. He showed us how to be, even when the encircling storms of wickedness swirl all around us. But not only did He show us how to be, He stands ready—today, right now—to help us to be and to become even as He is. We need not confront our own Judases without divine help and enabling, ennobling grace.

> Not only did Christ show us how to be, he stands ready—today, right now—to help us to become even as He is.

At the conclusion of the Last Supper, the Savior and His disciples joined in solemn singing before departing for the awful hours to be spent in Gethsemane. Knowing that these were to be the last mortal moments with those He called His friends, Jesus was both terse and tender in his instructions to the remaining

Apostles. Peter in particular was about to undergo a wrenching but important moment in His ministry. The Lord here models for us once again the way we must be, even during moments of high mental or emotional strain. When the seas of life are calm and the skies above us are clear, it is usually easier to be as we should be. But things were anything but calm on this night of nights. This was the night for which the Savior had been born. This was the grim culmination of His mortal mission, the purpose for which He had been prepared from the foundation of the world. Even still, He was, as always, focused on those around Him.

Christ here warns Peter that before the night's events had come to a climax he would three times deny that he knew the Savior. Peter's heart almost burst in protest. How could such a thing even be imagined? Did not his Master know by now of the depth of his loyalty? Hadn't he proven himself, again and again? Surely this was some final test, a painful but necessary way for the Lord to assess, one final time, the commitment of His chief Apostle. Even still, it must have come as a terrible shock to Peter to once again be singled out with such a dire forewarning. But the evening's events would soon show the wisdom of the Savior's words. Perhaps there was also some comfort to Peter in the fact that Jesus knew what would happen long before the cock crowed three times, yet He continued to mentor and encourage and love this as-yet-incomplete man of God.

In referencing the moment when Peter "comes to himself" after denying his relationship with the Savior for the third time, we're told that "Peter went out, and wept bitterly" (Matthew 26:75). Elder Gordon B. Hinckley likens this story to those of us who may also undergo a moment of moral wavering:

> As I have read this account my heart goes out to Peter. So many of us are so much like him. We pledge our loyalty; we affirm our determination to be of good courage; we declare, sometimes

> even publicly, that come what may we will do the right thing, that we will stand for the right cause, that we will be true to ourselves and to others.
>
> Then the pressures begin to build. Sometimes these are social pressures. Sometimes they are personal appetites. Sometimes they are false ambitions. There is a weakening of the will. There is a softening of discipline. There is capitulation. And then there is remorse, self-accusation, and bitter tears of regret. ("And Peter Went Out and Wept Bitterly," *Ensign*, May 1979, 63)

My purpose in recounting this story of Peter's denial is not to bring attention to Peter's flawed character. He was a remarkable man, one of the greatest to ever walk the earth. As we learn from the scriptures, the events following the death and Resurrection of the Lord would include Peter's fearless defense of the Church in spite of being beaten and imprisoned repeatedly. His valiance would ultimately lead to His also being crucified because he would not deny his testimony of the risen Redeemer. Peter endured to the end. Of that there is no question. The point of recounting this lowest of moments in Peter's life is to show how the Savior consistently responded to Peter's faults and flaws: With "loving kindness and long-suffering" (1 Nephi 19:9).

He looks on each of us in the same way and with the same loving, kind eyes as those that gazed at Peter in a moment of supreme emotional duress. Through his faith in the enabling grace of the Savior, Peter overcame his character flaws and became "a great benefit to his fellow beings" (Mosiah 8:18). We all have the potential to become what He would have us become and to respond to the strife and "ashes" of mortality even as He did.

Many other examples could be cited from the final hours of our Savior's mortal life that model how to respond to wickedness, even to wrenching and undeserved brutality. Whether referring to His unruffled silence in the courts of Annais, Caiaphas, Herod, and Pilate, or His meekness in receiving the mocking words, foul spittle, or vicious blows while blindfolded, His response was the same. Consider His astonishing plea to heaven to forgive those who were driving spikes into His tender hands, wrists, and feet, "for they know not what they do" (Luke 23:34). Consider Him hanging in unimaginable agony on the cross while delivering the tender injunction to John to take care of His mother, Mary. Try to comprehend Him reexperiencing, as Elder Bruce R. McConkie taught, all of the "infinite agonies and merciless pains of Gethsemane" again on the cross. Most poignantly, imagine Him suffering all of this alone, without even the comfort of His Father's immediate presence and soothing Spirit, the Holy Influence that had been with Him always.

In speaking of this moment, Elder Jeffrey R. Holland provided tender insight into this loneliest moment in the Savior's often-lonely life:

> Now I speak very carefully, even reverently, of what may have been the most difficult moment in all of this solitary journey to Atonement. I speak of those final moments for which Jesus must have been prepared intellectually and physically but which He may not have fully anticipated emotionally and spiritually—that concluding descent into the paralyzing despair of divine withdrawal when He cries in ultimate loneliness, "My God, my God, why hast thou forsaken me?" . . .
>
> [I]t is my personal belief that in all of Christ's mortal ministry the Father may never have been

> closer to His Son than in these agonizing final moments of suffering. Nevertheless, that the supreme sacrifice of His Son might be as complete as it was voluntary and solitary, the Father briefly withdrew from Jesus the comfort of His Spirit, the support of His personal presence. It was required, indeed it was central to the significance of the Atonement, that this perfect Son who had never spoken ill nor done wrong nor touched an unclean thing had to know how the rest of humankind—us, all of us—would feel when we did commit such sins. For His Atonement to be infinite and eternal, He had to feel what it was like to die not only physically but spiritually, to sense what it was like to have the divine Spirit withdraw, leaving one feeling totally, abjectly, hopelessly alone. ("None Were with Him," *Ensign*, May 2009, 87–88)

As Elder Holland reminds us, even discussing this event must be done carefully and reverently. The intimate relationship between the Father and the Son is so sacred, so tender, and so holy as to be considered, spiritually speaking, only on bended knee and with bowed head. But it is imperative that we understand, even in a limited way, that even in His moment of greatest heartbreak, Jesus Christ was thinking not of Himself but of you and of me. He was able to do this not only because of who He was but also because of whose He was. As spirit children of the same loving Heavenly Father, we too have access to the Light by which the Lord lived His sinless, selfless life. We too can become "beauty for ashes," even as the Savior showed us.

One final story from His life may give us additional hope to believe that there is hope regardless of how wounded our hearts may be. It is the account of His healing the woman with the issue of blood. I include two of the three Gospel accounts here because of the insights that each one provides in this small but meaningful moment in the Savior's ministry. Both accounts mention that Jesus has just been approached by a man named Jairus, one of the rulers of the synagogue, who pleads with the Lord to come and lay His hands on the man's dying daughter. Apparently there are many gathered around Him, wanting a blessing or a precious moment of personal attention. As He follows Jairus to his home, with many still "thronging" him, there is one in the crowd who watches Him pass with both hope and despair.

> And a certain woman, which had an issue of blood twelve years,
>
> And had suffered many things of many physicians, and had spent all that she had, and was nothing bettered, but rather grew worse,
>
> When she had heard of Jesus, came in the press behind, and touched his garment.
>
> For she said, If I may touch but his clothes, I shall be whole.
>
> And straightway the fountain of her blood was dried up; and she felt in her body that she was healed of that plague.
>
> And Jesus, immediately knowing in himself that virtue had gone out of him, turned him about in the press, and said, Who touched my clothes?
>
> And his disciples said unto him, Thou seest the multitude thronging thee, and sayest thou, Who touched me?
>
> And he looked round about to see her that had done this thing.
>
> But the woman fearing and trembling, knowing what was done in her, came and fell down before him, and told him all the truth.

> And he said unto her, Daughter, thy faith hath made thee whole; go in peace, and be whole of thy plague. (Mark 5:25–34)

Then from Luke we learn,

> And a woman having an issue of blood twelve years, which had spent all her living upon physicians, neither could be healed of any,
>
> Came behind him, and touched the border of his garment: and immediately her issue of blood stanched.
>
> And Jesus said, Who touched me? When all denied, Peter and they that were with him said, Master, the multitude throng thee and press thee, and sayest thou, Who touched me?
>
> And Jesus said, Somebody hath touched me: for I perceive that virtue is gone out of me.
>
> And when the woman saw that she was not hid, she came trembling, and falling down before him, she declared unto him before all the people for what cause she had touched him, and how she was healed immediately.
>
> And he said unto her, Daughter, be of good comfort: thy faith hath made thee whole; go in peace. (Luke 8:43–47)

Although it is likely we've read or heard this story recounted many times, there is a message relating directly to our relationships with each other and with the Savior that we may have overlooked in our previous study. In this brief and poignant moment, shared in three of the four Gospel accounts, we are once again reminded that Jesus was always looking for opportunities

Faith in the virtue of the Atonement is faith that will make us whole.

to minister to the one. Even when he was en route to provide healing to one, he didn't hesitate to stop and take the time needed to heal another. More important, in this story we are reminded that faith in the virtue of the Atonement is faith that will make us whole. This wholeness encompasses the healing we anxiously yearn for in our relationships. For twelve long years this dear woman had suffered, through no fault of her own, with a debilitating and humiliating medical condition. But as the scriptures relate, "she had spent all that she had, and was nothing bettered, but rather grew worse."

We may also make sincere attempts at bringing healing into our wounded and fractured relationships, but instead of improving, the rift between us widens. We too may expend great resources, even all that we have, in an effort to bring about "at one ment" with an estranged brother or sister only to see our strivings go for naught. In this brief moment in the life of our Savior, we find the Way forward. Just as this good woman came to the Lord with the simple faith that if she would but touch His robe and be made whole, so we too, when the pain is sufficiently searing, must likewise come to Him with faith to be healed. The virtue available to us is the same virtue that made this woman whole. We too must come "trembling, and falling down before him." I don't know how Jesus heals us, but I do know that He does heal. As far as we know, this woman had not had any previous interaction with the Savior. Mark tells us only that she had heard of Jesus and felt moved by simple faith to seek Him out when the opportunity arose for her to do so. In other words, she didn't need to be a gospel scholar or "someone important" to believe that merely touching the hem of the Savior's robe would bring about her long sought-for healing. We too don't need to wait until our life's circumstances are "just right" before we extend our hand to touch His healing robes. As Nephi taught, "He inviteth them all to come unto him, and partake of his goodness; and *he denieth none that come unto him*, black and white, bond and free, male and female; and he remembereth the heathen; *and all are alike unto God*, both Jew and Gentile" (2 Nephi 26:33; emphasis added).

> There is great power in becoming "beauty for ashes." Is the process simple? Yes. Easy? Anything but.

Throughout this book I've tried to show that there is great power in becoming "beauty for ashes." From the moment He announced His mortal mission to the final, painful moments of that mission as He hung in agony on the cross, Jesus Christ showed us both whom we should be and how we can become. Is the process simple? Yes. Easy? Anything but.

Becoming Christlike is the most grueling, demanding, and at times even excruciating work of our existence. Many setbacks and stumbles are to be expected. The shaping of our character and ultimately our very nature is what we are here to do. The power of becoming like Him is reflected in how we respond to the way we are treated by those around us. The confirmation of that influence may not always be immediately seen, but it will always be felt within the hearts of those to whom we give "beauty."

A simple example from the life of President George Albert Smith captures this principle beautifully. His granddaughter recounted the experience:

> Once on a hot summer day there was some problem happening under the street near Grandfather's home in Salt Lake City, and some workers from the city had come to fix it. It was hot outdoors, the sun shone fiercely, and the job at hand was a pick-and-shovel kind that made the sweat pour off the men's faces and backs as they dug into the roadway. The workers were not careful with their language, or maybe their mothers hadn't taught them any better, but they were swearing and using terrible language. Their words soon became offensive to many of the neighbors whose windows were open to catch any breeze that might help to cool them.
>
> Someone went out and asked the men to stop their foul talk, and in the process pointed out that Brother Smith lived right there—couldn't they show some respect and keep quiet, please? With that the men let loose a new string of bad words. Quietly, Grandfather prepared some lemonade and placing some glasses and the pitcher on a tray he carried it out to the struggling men with, 'My friends, you look so hot and tired. Why don't you come and sit under my trees here and have a cool drink?' Their anger gone, the men responded to the kindness with meekness and appreciation. After their pleasant little break they went back

> to their labor and finished their work carefully and quietly. ("The Power of Kindness," *Teachings of Presidents of the Church: George Albert Smith*, 2010, 223)

Without passing judgment on anyone else that could hear these men's language, isn't it interesting to reflect on how one person chose to respond to them? Rather than approaching them in a spirit of correction and anger, President Smith instead came to them with a gift and a sincere concern for their happiness. Not a word was spoken concerning their vulgarity. No words were needed. The power of his goodness softened their hearts far more effectively than any sermon he might have delivered. His sermon was a cold drink and the loving way in which it was given. His only agenda was love.

Jesus Christ changes hearts. It is what He died for. And it is what He lives for today.

Becoming "beauty for ashes" is a deeply demanding and breathtaking adventure of the soul. As with all things, the Savior can show us how. We need never face circumstances where we should return love for evil without His help and influence. He is able to provide us with the help we need "at all times and in all things, and in all places . . . even until death" (Mosiah 18:9) if we believe He can. Loving and doing good to our enemies is possible only if our hearts are changed.

Jesus Christ changes hearts. It is what He died for. And it is what He lives for today. Invite Him into your heart; invite Him to heal all of your heartaches. His example invites us to become the Christlike response. His infinite, intimate Atonement makes such a response possible. What could be more beautiful?

ABOUT THE AUTHOR

SCOTT LIVINGSTON WASN'T BORN TO be a writer. He was born to be Ginger's husband. The writing thing happened as the result of his winning a writing contest in the fourth grade that involved describing what he'd do if he was the strongest man in the world. Something about uprooting trees with his bare hands. It was fourth grade, people.

He has since had the privilege of becoming a dad, a teacher, and one that seems to have hit the "I live around amazing people" jackpot. He loves making up stories of all kinds, and occasionally even writing movies too.

If something he writes reminds you that you are amazing . . . Mission Accomplished.